Leo Tolstoy: A Very Short Introduction

VERY SHORT INTRODUCTIONS are for anyone wanting a stimulating and accessible way into a new subject. They are written by experts, and have been translated into more than 45 different languages.

The series began in 1995, and now covers a wide variety of topics in every discipline. The VSI library currently contains over 600 volumes—a Very Short Introduction to everything from Psychology and Philosophy of Science to American History and Relativity—and continues to grow in every subject area.

Very Short Introductions available now:

ABOLITIONISM Richard S. Newman
ACCOUNTING Christopher Nobes
ADAM SMITH Christopher J. Berry
ADOLESCENCE Peter K. Smith
ADVERTISING Winston Fletcher
AFRICAN AMERICAN RELIGION
    Eddie S. Glaude Jr
AFRICAN HISTORY John Parker
    and Richard Rathbone
AFRICAN POLITICS Ian Taylor
AFRICAN RELIGIONS
    Jacob K. Olupona
AGEING Nancy A. Pachana
AGNOSTICISM Robin Le Poidevin
AGRICULTURE Paul Brassley
    and Richard Soffe
ALEXANDER THE GREAT
    Hugh Bowden
ALGEBRA Peter M. Higgins
AMERICAN CULTURAL HISTORY
    Eric Avila
AMERICAN HISTORY Paul S. Boyer
AMERICAN IMMIGRATION
    David A. Gerber
AMERICAN LEGAL HISTORY
    G. Edward White
AMERICAN NAVAL HISTORY
    Craig L. Symonds
AMERICAN POLITICAL HISTORY
    Donald Critchlow
AMERICAN POLITICAL PARTIES
    AND ELECTIONS L. Sandy Maisel
AMERICAN POLITICS
    Richard M. Valelly

THE AMERICAN PRESIDENCY
    Charles O. Jones
THE AMERICAN REVOLUTION
    Robert J. Allison
AMERICAN SLAVERY
    Heather Andrea Williams
THE AMERICAN WEST Stephen Aron
AMERICAN WOMEN'S HISTORY
    Susan Ware
ANAESTHESIA Aidan O'Donnell
ANALYTIC PHILOSOPHY
    Michael Beaney
ANARCHISM Colin Ward
ANCIENT ASSYRIA Karen Radner
ANCIENT EGYPT Ian Shaw
ANCIENT EGYPTIAN ART AND
    ARCHITECTURE Christina Riggs
ANCIENT GREECE Paul Cartledge
THE ANCIENT NEAR EAST
    Amanda H. Podany
ANCIENT PHILOSOPHY Julia Annas
ANCIENT WARFARE
    Harry Sidebottom
ANGELS David Albert Jones
ANGLICANISM Mark Chapman
THE ANGLO-SAXON AGE John Blair
ANIMAL BEHAVIOUR
    Tristram D. Wyatt
THE ANIMAL KINGDOM
    Peter Holland
ANIMAL RIGHTS David DeGrazia
THE ANTARCTIC Klaus Dodds
ANTHROPOCENE Erle C. Ellis
ANTISEMITISM Steven Beller

Available soon:

For more information visit our website

www.oup.com/vsi/

Liza Knapp

LEO TOLSTOY

A Very Short Introduction

OXFORD
UNIVERSITY PRESS

OXFORD
UNIVERSITY PRESS

Great Clarendon Street, Oxford, OX2 6DP,
United Kingdom

Oxford University Press is a department of the University of Oxford.
It furthers the University's objective of excellence in research, scholarship,
and education by publishing worldwide. Oxford is a registered trade mark of
Oxford University Press in the UK and in certain other countries

© Liza Knapp 2019

The moral rights of the author have been asserted

First edition published in 2019

Impression: 1

Published in the United States of America by Oxford University Press
198 Madison Avenue, New York, NY 10016, United States of America

British Library Cataloguing in Publication Data
Data available

Library of Congress Control Number: 2019933929

ISBN 978-0-19-881393-4

Printed in Great Britain by
Ashford Colour Press Ltd, Gosport, Hampshire

Links to third party websites are provided by Oxford in good faith and
for information only. Oxford disclaims any responsibility for the materials
contained in any third party website referenced in this work.

Contents

Acknowledgements

It's a challenge to write a very short introduction to Tolstoy; I am grateful to the people who helped me. I wish to thank Andrea Keegan, Jenny Nugee, and others at Oxford University Press for their guidance and insight, and the outside readers for their advice. For their wise and clear-sighted judgement on how to make this introduction very short and more direct I thank Lauren Horst and Milan Terlunen.

Exploring the labyrinths of Tolstoy's novels on my own and in the classroom has been a joy for me. The questions about love, death, peace, war, faith, social justice, human rights, and art that Tolstoy addresses in his novels animate all that he wrote and did. I marvel at the different ways that Tolstoy inspires and provokes his public. And I am indebted to students, teachers, colleagues, scholars, friends, loved ones, and strangers who over the years have shared with me their responses to Tolstoy and the questions he asks.

Publication of this book was made possible, in part, with a grant from the Harriman Institute, Columbia University.

Note on references to Tolstoy's works

I cite from the following translations of Tolstoy's works, with occasional changes in wording. In parentheses after the quotation or reference, I give the chapter numbers (if the work is divided into chapters), followed by the page numbers of these particular editions. For *Anna Karenina* and *Resurrection*, I give part number, chapter number, and then page number. For *War and Peace*, I give book, part, and chapter numbers, followed by page numbers. For Tolstoy's journals and letters (unless otherwise noted), I give the volume and page numbers for references to the 90-volume complete works of Tolstoy in Russian (Tolstoi, Lev., *Polnoe sobranie sochinenii*, 90 vols. Moscow: Khudozhestvennaia literatura, 1928–58).

'Alyosha Pot', in *The Death of Ivan Ilyich and Other Stories*, trans. Nicolas Pasternak Slater (Oxford: Oxford World's Classics, 2015), 149–54.

Anna Karenina, trans. Rosamund Bartlett (Oxford: Oxford World's Classics, 2014).

Childhood, Boyhood, Youth, trans. Judson Rosengrant (London: Penguin, 2012).

Confession, in *A Confession, The Gospel in Brief, and What I Believe*, trans. Aylmer Maude (London: Oxford World's Classics, 1971), pp. 1–84.

'Death of Ivan Ilyich', *The Death of Ivan Ilyich and Other Stories*, trans. Nicolas Pasternak Slater (Oxford: Oxford World's Classics, 2015), 149–54.

The Gospel in Brief, in *A Confession, The Gospel in Brief, and What I Believe*, trans. Aylmer Maude (London, Oxford World's Classics, 1971), pp. 96–302.

Hadji Murat [*Hadji Murad*], in *The Kreutzer Sonata and Other Stories*, trans. Aylmer Maude, Louise Maude, and J. D. Duff (Oxford: Oxford World's Classics, 2009), pp. 344–467.

'I Cannot Be Silent', *Recollections and Essays*, trans. Aylmer and Louise Maude (London: Oxford University Press, 1937), pp. 395–412.

The Kingdom of God Is Within You: Christianity Not as a Mystic Religion but as a New Theory of Life, trans. Constance Garnett (Lincoln, Nebr.: University of Nebraska Press, 1984).

'The Kreutzer Sonata', *The Kreutzer Sonata and Other Stories*, trans. Aylmer Maude, Louise Maude, and J. D. Duff (Oxford: Oxford World's Classics, 2009), pp. 85–177.

'Need It Be So?' in *The Complete Works of Count Tolstoy: Miscellaneous Letters and Essays*, trans. Leo Wiener (Boston: Dana Estes, 1905).

'The Raid', *The Raid and Other Stories*, trans. Louise and Aylmer Maude (Oxford: Oxford World's Classics, 1982), pp. 1–28.

Resurrection, trans. Louise Maude (Oxford: Oxford World's Classics, 1994).

'Sevastopol in December', 'Sevastopol in May', 'Sevastopol in August 1855', *Collected Shorter Fiction*, trans. Louise and Aylmer Maude (New York: Knopf, 2001), 1:81–204.

War and Peace, trans. Louise and Aylmer Maude, rev. Amy Mandelker (Oxford: Oxford World's Classics, 2010).

What I Believe, in *A Confession, The Gospel in Brief, and What I Believe*, trans. Aylmer Maude (London: Oxford World's Classics, 1971), pp. 303–539.

What Then Must We Do?, The Works of Leo Tolstoy, trans. Aylmer Maude, introd. Jane Addams (London: Oxford University Press, 1934), vol. 14.

List of illustrations

Chapter 1

From Ant Brothers to loving all as brothers and sisters

Tolstoy as writer, thinker, man

In our day, Leo Tolstoy is known as the author of *War and Peace* and *Anna Karenina*, two of the greatest novels ever written; as the father of the modern war story; as an innovator in psychological prose and forerunner of stream of consciousness; as a master of rendering the child's point of view; as a virtuoso at revealing human character; as a genius at using fiction to reveal the mysteries of love and death; and as a writer who never tired of asking 'why live?'

At the time of his death in 1910, Tolstoy was known the world over as a great writer *and* as a voice of protest. He was a merciless critic of institutions that perpetrated, bred, or tolerated injustice, hatred, and violence in any form. Tolstoy devoted the last decades of his life to posing—and attempting to answer—more directly the very questions that had animated his famous fiction. To this end, he wrote works with strikingly direct titles: 'What I Believe', 'The Gospels in Brief', 'What Then Must We Do?', 'How Much Land Does a Person Need?', 'The Kingdom of God Is Within You', 'What Is Art?', 'Bethink Yourselves', 'I Cannot Be Silent'. These later works expand on and confirm insights that Tolstoy had already revealed in his fiction.

1

Among literary critics and rival writers, it has been a commonplace to disparage Tolstoy's 'thought' while praising his 'art'. The practice of bashing Tolstoy the thinker dates back at least to French novelist Gustave Flaubert, who complained to his Russian friend and fellow novelist Ivan Turgenev after reading *War and Peace* that Tolstoy was a great psychologist and artist, but a bad philosopher. Among American writers, Ernest Hemingway praised Tolstoy for capturing the truth about war better than anyone, but also claimed *War and Peace* would have been so much better (and shorter) if written by Turgenev. Hemingway also complained of Tolstoy's 'ponderous and Messianic thinking'. Mark Twain's notebooks contain a brief comment to the effect that he must 'bring down Tolstoy', which is thought to be a response to a comment made by William Dean Howells to the effect that 'an average American humorist could dispose of [Tolstoy's] arguments in a half-column funny article'. (Mark Twain was getting ready to rise to this challenge.) But what's important here is that while Howells, who did so much to popularize Tolstoy in the United States, can't resist inserting the quip about how easy and fun it would be to 'dispose of [Tolstoy's] arguments', the rest of the article expresses his genuine awe at Tolstoy's way of 'not relegat[ing] the practice of the Christian life to some future period, but himself attempt[ing] it here and now'. Howells observes that it is Tolstoy's 'conscience' that makes his fiction great and that if it 'has now changed from a dramatic to a hortatory expression', 'the same good heart and right mind are under all and in all'.

One of the aims of this Very Short Introduction is to convince you that Tolstoy's art and thought aren't separable, and that knowing more about his thought enriches our understanding of his fiction.

Ant Brothers and the green stick

Tolstoy was born and lived most of his life at Yasnaya Polyana, a family estate in the Tula province, about 125 miles south of

1. Leo Tolstoy at Yasnaya Polyana in a photograph by his wife Sophia.

Moscow (Figure 1). Late in life, Tolstoy recalled how in their childhood his oldest brother Nikolai came up with a game that became a favourite for Tolstoy and his siblings, who were then motherless and soon to be fatherless. It was called Ant Brothers. How do you play Ant Brothers? The Tolstoy children would drape shawls between chairs and use pillows and boxes to create a protective shelter in which they would become Ant Brothers, snuggling together and experiencing 'a special feeling of love and tenderness'. Nikolai also told them that, buried somewhere at Yasnaya Polyana, was a green stick. And on this green stick was inscribed the secret that would reveal 'what had to be done' so that 'all people would become happy, there would be no sickness, no trouble, no adversity, and nobody would feel anger for anyone, and everyone would love one another: all would become "ant brothers"' (34:386).

Looking back, Tolstoy explained that his brother must have heard about the Moravian Brothers, a counter-cultural group of Protestants who practised and spread Jesus's teachings of love.

3

The Moravian Brothers set up missionary colonies in various lands. And since in Russian the words for ant and for Moravian sound a lot alike, Tolstoy's brother somehow conflated the two. Tolstoy further surmised that his brother had heard their father and others talk about the Brotherhood of Freemasons with their efforts at 'making mankind happy' and their 'mystic initiation rituals'. The game of Ant Brothers took inspiration from real-life efforts at spreading brotherly love.

All his life, Tolstoy cherished his childhood dream 'of ant brothers lovingly cleaving to each other, only not between two chairs, draped with shawls, but of all the people of the world under the whole wide cope of heaven' (34:387). Tolstoy came to see the love he felt while playing Ant Brothers as his first religious experience: the love was 'not love for someone, but love for love, love for God'. He declared that what he and his siblings 'had called a game' was in fact the only thing on earth that was not a game (34:392).

He held on to his faith: 'just as I believed then that there was that green stick on which was written what would destroy all evil in people and give them great happiness, so do I now believe that this truth exists and that it will be revealed to people.' The game of Ant Brothers and the green stick contains in concentrated form many of the hallmarks of Tolstoy's thought and art: the yearning for universal love, the aversion to violence and war, the transformation of the everyday world through imagination, the search for human comfort in the shadow of death. That the credo that Tolstoy later formulated took root in this childhood game is proof of the continuity and unity in Tolstoy's work. And all his fiction, from *Childhood, Boyhood, Youth* and early war stories, through the great novels, to his later stories, shows that their author remained true to his childhood ideal of the Ant Brothers and the green stick. It is impossible to separate his art from the values embodied in this game.

Ant Brothers in *Childhood*

In key moments in his fiction, Tolstoy imparted to his heroes variants of what the motherless Tolstoy siblings experienced as Ant Brothers beneath the shelter of shawls. Barricaded off from the rest of the world, these characters feel love and tenderness, but also want all others, in the world beyond, to somehow feel the same.

In a chapter called 'Childhood' within the first part of Tolstoy's trilogy *Childhood, Boyhood, Youth*, the narrator Nikolai Irtenev, who is 10 when the action begins, recalls an earlier period of childhood when he was very small. In the flashback, little Nikolai, about to go to bed, declares his love for his mother, then prays to God, noting that his love for his mother and his love for God 'somehow became strangely fused into a single feeling'. Then, as he's falling asleep, he remembers his tutor, 'the only unhappy person [he] knew', and prays that God make his tutor happy and wonders what he, Nikolai, can do. The sleepy prayer trails off as Nikolai prays 'for God to grant happiness to all, for everyone to be content, and for good weather' the next day (15, 55–6).

This 'happy' childhood memory has many of the components of Tolstoy's own game of Ant Brothers: snuggled in bed, Tolstoy's young hero feels the kind of love and religious feeling that Tolstoy experienced huddled with his siblings as they played Ant Brothers. But little Nikolai Irtenev, like Tolstoy, recalls the sorrow and trouble of others and wants them to be happy too. He wants that green stick.

Ant Brothers at the siege of Sevastopol

Tolstoy's Sevastopol tales, which caused a literary sensation during and after the Crimean War, show that this childhood game of Ant Brothers—with that green stick yet to be found—haunted and inspired his war stories too. 'Sevastopol in August' follows Vladimir Kozeltsov, an ensign, fresh from military academy in Petersburg, as he reports to duty in the besieged city. With a head full of clichéd fantasies of heroic action ahead, he is charged with leading a group of men. They spend the night in a dug-out shelter on the bastions and anticipate action the next day, which, as it turns out, is the day Sevastopol will fall and Kozeltsov will be killed.

What Kozeltsov feels among these men in the shelter is 'a sensation of coziness such as he had felt as a child when, playing hide-and-seek, he used to creep into a cupboard or under his mother's skirt' (21,189). Like the motherless Tolstoy children as they played Ant Brothers, young Kozeltsov has been forever exiled from his mother's protective embrace. (He remembers how as they parted his mother tearfully prayed before an icon.) But, in this new band of brothers in the dark shelter, he feels an 'uncanny' tenderness and exaltation that replaces the more familiar forms of familial, romantic, and religious love.

That this takes place on the bastion in time of war and on the eve of Kozeltsov's death is Tolstoy's irony and agony: here are these men feeling brotherhood and loving one another, but about to kill or be killed by other men when the sun rises over Sevastopol in the morning. What is the point? Where is the green stick that would reveal the mystery of how to draw *all people* under the cope of heaven together in love, and put an end to enmity? Here, as elsewhere in his fiction, Tolstoy plants allusions to that green stick and then shows life going on. Later in life Tolstoy would preach more directly about beating swords into ploughshares.

Ant Brothers among prisoners in *War and Peace*

In *War and Peace* (1869), Tolstoy's epic set during the Napoleonic wars (1803–15), Pierre Bezukhov is captured and tried by the French as they besiege a burning Moscow. Pierre witnesses the execution of some of his fellow prisoners, believing that his turn is next. Although Pierre is spared at the last minute, the executions he witnesses leave him bereft of faith in the goodness of the world order, of humanity, of his soul, and of God. This marks a dramatic change in Pierre who, by temperament, is drawn to the dream of universal Ant-Brotherly love. At the start of *War and Peace*, Pierre reveals his dreams of a world without war; a quest for universal brotherhood embroils him with the Freemasons.

After viewing the executions, Pierre spends the next month in a shed with twenty other prisoners of war, including Platon Karataev, a serf conscript in the Russian army. Platon's love—for 'his dog, his comrades, the French, and Pierre who was his neighbor' in the shed—is unlike any Pierre has known (4.1:13, 1047). But it resembles the love that Tolstoy ascribed to himself and his siblings as they cleaved together as Ant Brothers in their shelter: their love was 'not love for someone [in particular], but love for love, love for God'. The fact that Platon Karataev's love includes the French—that is, the enemy—suggests that he may in fact be revealing what was on that green stick: a love that includes all and knows no distinctions. In Tolstoy's 'Gospel in Brief' and elsewhere in his later religious writings, Tolstoy would emphasize the fact that your 'neighbour' is not just your 'fellow countryman' (9, 230). Love your neighbour means love everybody.

Under these special circumstances as a prisoner of war for those thirty days and nights with Platon Karataev as his neighbour, Pierre comes to feel a new, unknown feeling of joy, tranquillity, love, and strength. However, when the French evacuate Moscow and the Russian prisoners are forced to march on foot, relations both among prisoners and between them and the French change from friendliness to enmity. The French execute anyone they deem to be unfit for the march. Thus, when Platon falls sick and beckons Pierre over for a wordless farewell, Pierre pretends not to notice and walks by. Shortly after, Pierre hears the shot and sees the French soldiers hurrying away after killing Platon. Tolstoy explains that Pierre's denial of Platon somehow seemed necessary to his own survival: he 'was not sufficiently sure of himself' (4.3:14, 1144–5). The memory of Platon's life inspires Pierre hereafter. Still, for many readers, Pierre's refusal to draw near to Platon is one of the cruellest moments in Tolstoy's work.

Levin's estate as a shelter in *Anna Karenina*

At the end of *Anna Karenina*, after the death of Anna, Tolstoy provides an epilogue-like eighth part, devoted largely to the other central plot of the novel, that of Levin and Kitty. Levin has been suffering a spiritual crisis that leaves him, 'a happy family man', faithful husband, and conscientious landowner, close to suicide. But, on the last day of the action of the novel, Levin reaffirms his faith in God and is restored to life. Levin concludes that he has been 'living well but thinking badly' (8:12, 801). He has attempted to create on his family estate a safe and loving zone, which recalls, in some respects, the shelter created by the Tolstoy children when they pretended to be Ant Brothers. The estate is aptly named Pokrovskoe: the Russian root (*pokrov*) means 'shelter' and this name evokes the protective veil of the Mother of God (Russian Orthodox Christians pray for its protection). As Tolstoy described it, 'being ant brothers...meant only to curtain ourselves off from everyone, to separate ourselves from everyone and everything and to love one another' (33:391–2). In *Anna Karenina*, this is what Levin does. At Pokrovskoe, Levin isolates himself with his extended family, in a realm where he cultivates this love.

But as *Anna Karenina* ends, family happiness is troubled by questions about the plight of those beyond the family circle. How far should love of neighbour extend? As Levin and his loved ones gather by the beehives Levin has been cultivating, eating cucumbers and honey, they debate the pros and cons of humanitarian military intervention in the Balkans: should Russia come to the aid of their fellow Slavs who are suffering under Ottoman rule? Vronsky has been seen heading off to join Russian volunteers. Levin argues for staying home on the grounds that he feels no particular neighbourly love for the Serbs: war is serious business and he asks whether killing to protect a victim is even justified.

Levin's questions about the use of violence, even under these circumstances, look ahead to the full-scale rejection of violence, even in cases of defending victims, that was to be one of the most contentious aspects of Tolstoy's later doctrine of non-violence (see Chapter 5, 'Non-violence in Gethsemane, at Yasnaya Polyana and beyond'). Meanwhile, in *Diary of a Writer*, fellow novelist Dostoevsky ridiculed Levin for his isolationism—for caring about Kitty's appetite and their baby's bath while apparently feeling nothing for mothers and children suffering in the Balkans.

But even as Levin curtains himself off with his loved ones in the shelter of his family estate, he still bears others in mind, much as the Ant Brothers did when they dreamed of the happiness of all. At the very end of *Anna Karenina*, after Kitty and their baby narrowly miss being killed when an oak is struck by lightning, Levin rejoices in his love for his family, safe and sound at Pokrovskoe. But he also has, on that very day, renewed faith after a desperate spiritual struggle.

Levin reasons that affirming his faith in the Christian law that he had 'imbibed with his mother's milk' united him, 'whether [he] like[d] it or not, in one congregation of believers which is called the Church' (8:12, 801; 8:19, 820). This, however, makes him uneasy. Levin asks himself, as he gazes up at the cope of heaven, what about those of other faiths 'who also are reverent and do good'? Would God have denied 'revelation of what is good' and salvation to 'Jews, Muslims, Confucians, Buddhists'? (8:18–19, 818–20). These questions as the novel closes hint that Levin will not be content to play at Ant Brothers at Pokrovskoe. He, like Tolstoy, wants to find that green stick and will search on. But, as the starry skies confirm for Levin God's presence in the universe,

Levin surrenders, at least for this summer's night, to God's infinite goodness and wisdom, and affirms that he, Levin, has the power to instil goodness in his life (8:19, 822).

Ant Brothers in the real world

Tolstoy continued to write, live, and work in hope of the truth being revealed that would enact brotherly love and put an end to enmity in the world beyond the Ant Brothers' shelter, beyond Kozeltsov's shelter at Sevastopol, beyond the shed Pierre shared with Platon and others, and beyond even Levin's estate of Pokrovskoe. In the works Tolstoy wrote about faith in the wake of *Anna Karenina*, he extracted from Jesus's Sermon on the Mount a social gospel of 'peace among men', of 'love for all', and of non-violence. In *What I Believe*, Tolstoy wrote that if people live accordingly, 'all men will be brothers, and everyone will be at peace with others, enjoying all the blessings of the world during the term of life appointed them by God. Men will beat their swords into ploughshares, and their spears into pruning-hooks' (6, 406). This was what the Ant Brothers had dreamed of and what Tolstoy believed in.

In 1902, Tolstoy, by then a voice of moral authority throughout the world—and a thorn in the side of the Russian government and Church—wrote a letter to Tsar Nicholas II, addressing him as 'Dear Brother'. Tolstoy explained that he used this unexpected form of address because he wrote to him 'not so much as a tsar' but 'as a man—a brother'. He explained that since he expected to die soon, he wrote 'as if from the other world' (73:184). (Although he was very ill at the time, he would in fact recover, and live and write for another eight years.) Tolstoy wrote from a zone in which divisions—of power, of class, of nation, of creed, of gender—that structure earthly life ceased to matter. All human beings were brothers and sisters.

In the letter, written as the unrest, which eventually led to the revolutions of 1905 and 1918, was growing, Tolstoy informed the tsar that autocracy was 'an obsolete form of government' unsuited to the needs of the Russian people. He warned the tsar that continuing his current actions would bring untold evil on the Russian people and himself. And, finally, he counselled the tsar on how to sow brotherhood. Tolstoy attempted to make the dream of the Ant Brothers into a political reality and to impart the secret inscribed on that green stick. Daring as this letter was, Tolstoy wrote it in the spirit of Ant Brothers: he wanted to include the tsar in the huddle and inspire him to act in a spirit of brotherly love for all. In this same spirit of brotherhood, Tolstoy corresponded with Mohandas Gandhi, recognizing in him someone committed to a similar ideal, as well as with countless others. Tolstoy still believed the dream of the Ant Brothers could come to fruition and did what he could to make that happen.

Chapter 2
Tolstoy on war and on peace

Tolstoy is often hailed as the father of the modern war story.
In the introduction to *Men at War,* an anthology of war stories
throughout history, Ernest Hemingway declared that 'there is no
better writing on war than there is in Tolstoy'. As Hemingway saw
it, 'a writer's job is to tell the truth'. What makes Tolstoy's writing
on war so good—and so modern—is how he seems to tell the
truth about war. Tolstoy pledged his allegiance to the truth at the
end of one of his early Crimean War stories, 'Sevastopol in May',
when he wrote: 'The hero of my tale—that I love with all the
power of my soul, that I have tried to portray in all his beauty, that
has been, is, and will be beautiful—is Truth' (16, 135). Tolstoy
made it his goal to tell true war stories. To do this, he needed to
break with convention.

Before declaring his 'hero' to be truth, Tolstoy had denied this
heroic status to participants in the war—even to one of the officers
known for his 'brilliant courage' and to another who died 'for faith,
for throne, and for fatherland'. In this act, Tolstoy made it clear
that he was not going to repeat old lies to the effect that 'it is sweet
and fitting to die for one's country'. Rather, Tolstoy admits that for
all the qualities that might make his characters heroic according
to the standard definitions of glory and heroism, they are all in
fact 'neither good, nor bad' and 'neither heroes, nor villains'.
These distinctions get blurred in war.

But Tolstoy went further in his truth-telling to reveal not just that war is hell, but that it violates the 'law of love' that the participants profess. In the final scene of 'Sevastopol in May', as friend and foe fraternize during a ceasefire called for the burial of a pile of corpses, Tolstoy asks, 'why do they not embrace like brothers with tears of joy and gladness', instead of starting to kill again in the morning? As in the game of Ant Brothers, Tolstoy believed that human beings were meant to love one another like brothers, not to kill each other. What are they fighting for?

The story goes on to suggest that this kind of truth-telling about war is too bitter for humankind to bear: in order to go about their business, in this case making war, human beings suppress these truths 'that lie unconsciously hidden in the soul of each man' (16, 137). Later in life, Tolstoy embraced these truths: he condemned war, preached non-violence, and rejected patriotism when it meant loving one's fellow-countrymen to the detriment of others.

When he began to write war stories as a young man, Tolstoy himself was not yet ready to lay down arms or break with the way of the world. And he wanted his works to be published, which, given the strict government censorship and the sensibility of the reading public, meant he could not present too bleak a view of Russia's wars. (Tolstoy bore these constraints in mind as he wrote and revised his works; and he often fumed when editors and censors made further changes.) Still, from his early war tales on, bitter truths and tough questions surface in key moments, even as he depicts officers fuelled by the ecstasy of war and dreams of glory or patriots defending their homeland. The pacifism that Tolstoy extolled in later non-fiction works has its seeds in his early fiction.

Tolstoy and his forerunners

As he modernized the war story, Tolstoy drew on a tradition extending from the ancient Greek epic poet Homer to his own day. Of his own epic novel *War and Peace*, Tolstoy once suggested to

the writer Maxim Gorky: 'without false modesty, it is like the Iliad'.
Like Tolstoy, Homer was especially interested in the interplay
between the realms of war and of peace. Homer's juxtapositions of
war and peace, whether in simile, in speech, in action, or in the
description of the shield of Achilles, are laced with a sense of
regret, possibly even protest.

The *Iliad* ends with a ceasefire bringing together in a moment of
mutual understanding two enemies: the Greek warrior Achilles
and the Trojan king Priam, father of the slain warrior Hector.
After brutalizing Hector's body, Achilles, feeling compassion for
the grieving Priam, agrees to surrender the body for burial.
Women lament. This scene looks ahead to memorable scenes in
Tolstoy's war stories when enemies cease to care about glory or
country and recognize the brother in their enemy. But the *Iliad*
also makes it clear that the killing will start up again. Wrath has
not been eradicated. War will go on. Even as he celebrates the
valour of those who fight, Homer reveals the sorrow of war.

Closer to his time, Tolstoy recognized French novelist Stendhal as
his most immediate literary model for deromanticizing war and
describing it as it really is. As one French critic noted, Stendhal was
able to give a more 'truthful' account of what really happens in war
in part because he lacked convictions. Stendhal made it hard for
other writers to return to epic modes of telling war stories. In *The
Charterhouse of Parma* (1839), Stendhal presents the Battle of
Waterloo at it was experienced by a novice to war, Fabrice del
Dongo. By battle's end, 'War was no longer that noble endeavor
shared by all those who love glory that he had imagined it to be
from reading the proclamations of Napoleon!' Tolstoy remarked on
the effectiveness of using Fabrice, a novice at war, who goes through
the battle and 'understands nothing' to represent war 'as it really is'.

Tolstoy became a virtuoso of this mode of depicting warfare
from the point of view of a naive observer and also adapted it to
portraying the opera and other experiences (see Chapter 7,

'Defamiliarization or "looking at things afresh"'). In a famous segment of *War and Peace*, the Battle of Borodino is depicted from the point of view of Pierre Bezukhov, a novice to war, who bumbles onto the battlefield and gets caught up in combat (Figure 2). Tolstoy uses this device to reveal the same cynical truth about war as Stendhal, but Tolstoy makes it his own when he shows Pierre's moral horror. Tolstoy's Pierre "understands nothing'—except that everyone ought to 'be horrified at what they have done' and stop (3.2:33, 857).

2. **Pierre Bezukhov at the Battle of Borodino in *War and Peace*, illustration by Dementy Shmarinov.**

Warfare in the Caucasus

Tolstoy's first experience of war was in the Caucasus, a mountainous region between the Black and the Caspian seas, where the Russian Empire had been fighting for decades to conquer and subdue the local peoples. In 1851, when he was 23, Tolstoy set off for Chechnya with his oldest brother Nikolai, whose battalion was stationed there. Tolstoy ended up staying in the region for three years, at first without an official position, then as a cadet in the Russian artillery.

When he set off for the Caucasus, Tolstoy was starting to become serious about writing. He was at work on *Childhood*, which was published in 1852. He continued to write about the life of the Russian gentry back in Russia and wrote *Boyhood* and *Youth* to create a trilogy. To this domestic subject matter Tolstoy now added the Russian conquest of the Caucasus, which had been popular with his Romantic predecessors, including Pushkin, Lermontov, and others. In the course of his life, he wrote several war stories set in the Caucasus, among them, 'The Raid' (1853), *The Cossacks* (not finished until 1862), 'The Prisoner of the Caucasus' (1872), and, later, *Hadji Murat* (published 1912).

In his first war story, 'The Raid: A Volunteer's Story' (1853), Tolstoy makes strategic use of the outsider status of a first-person narrator who tags along on a Russian raid on a Chechen village. This narrator can record devastating observations and express feelings that participants wouldn't. The volunteer wants to see 'action', to get a vicarious sense of 'the rapture' of war that grips some of the young officers, and to enjoy what he calls 'the spectacle'. But he declares 'the truly magnificent spectacle' 'spoilt' by the excessive histrionics of the cavalry as they gallop 'in a cloud of dust' and 'with a war cry' toward a village that the artillery has already bombarded. When a wounded man moans, he notes that 'no one except myself seems to notice it' and the 'war scene instantly lost its charm'. The captain in that battalion suspects him of just 'want[ing] to see how people get killed'. In the end, the volunteer stops short of reflecting too much either on his own desire to see violence or on the violence itself (1, 2; 10, 30; 8, 21; 1, 30). Tolstoy, however, has given the reader plenty to think about.

Tolstoy's narrator in 'The Raid' has a special way of describing nature and its inhabitants. At one point, as the hero of 'The Raid' listens to the night sounds while waiting for the Russian ambush of a village to begin, he refers to the 'ringing voices of the frogs' coming from the river. Tolstoy adds a footnote to say that 'Frogs in the Caucasus make a noise quite different from the croaking of frogs elsewhere.' However, Tolstoy isn't just after the local colour and realistic detail. The ringing of the frogs is part of a long sensual and meditative description of the night. The sounds of the natural world, which includes frogs, jackals, crickets, and quails, create a 'beautiful harmony', whereas human sounds—a barrel-organ grinding out 'some Aurora Waltz' (for the pleasure of the Russian conquerors), 'officers noisily giving orders', the 'clang of a heavy gun'—create noise.

In this environment, Tolstoy's narrator gazes at the 'immeasurable starry heavens' above him and wonders: 'Can it be possible that in the midst of this entrancing Nature feelings of hatred, vengeance, or the desire to exterminate their fellows, can endure in the souls of men?' The 'starry heavens' evoke the reaction of philosopher Immanuel Kant, who was filled with awe by starry skies above and moral law within him. Tolstoy's first war story, then, does double duty as a peace story: why do all not surrender to the 'pacifying beauty and power' of the starry skies above and listen to the frogs ring instead of killing?

In his Caucasian tales, Tolstoy and his heroes not only marvel at the natural world, they sometimes also show an interest in the peoples they encounter. Tolstoy wryly describes Russian officers who attempt to go native and imitate the Tatars (a Turkic-speaking people in the region) in everything from their dress to the way they sit on their horse. He suggests the potential for brotherly connection despite cultural differences, only to then remind readers of the political realities of imperial conquest. The question lurking in Tolstoy's Caucasian war stories is: how can the brotherhood of all people be possible in a political and social realm that operates according to principles antithetical to brotherhood?

When Tolstoy introduces a Tatar word, this detail, if only for a brief moment, conjures up the perspective of the local people whom the Russians are conquering. As 'dragoons, Cossacks, and infantry' survey with 'evident delight' the village they have ravaged, looking for spoils, a Cossack carries out a '*kumgan* of milk', takes a swig, and throws it down on the ground with a loud laugh (9, 22). Tolstoy clarifies in a footnote that *kumgan* means 'pitcher'. But, subtly, suddenly, Tolstoy invites the reader into the daily life of these inhabitants, which most of the Russian raiders ignore even as they violate it.

In *Hadji Murat*, his final Caucasian tale and his final war story, begun in 1896 but not published until after his death, Tolstoy returns to the subject matter of 'The Raid' as he describes the raid of a village in Chechnya from two different perspectives, that of the raiders and that of the raided. First, he follows the Russian raiders, taken as they are with 'a poetic conception of war' and oblivious to the damage and suffering they inflict (16, 424). Then, in the next chapter, the inhabitants of the village return to find their homes burned, their crops destroyed, their mosque desecrated, their water source befouled.

Whereas the first-person narrator of 'The Raid' had to stick to what he observed, the narrator in *Hadji Murat* ranges freely through space to describe different scenes, and reads the minds and hearts of a large variety of characters, from Nicholas, tsar of

Russia, and Shamil, imam of Chechnya, down to the inhabitants of the raided village. (As he wrote *Hadji Murat*, Tolstoy took liberties that he did not take in his youth.) Here is what Tolstoy imagines to be the villagers' response to the Russian raid:

> The feeling experienced by all the Chechens, from the youngest to the oldest, was stronger than hate. It was not hatred, for they did not regard those Russian dogs as human beings, but it was such repulsion, disgust, and perplexity at the senseless cruelty of these creatures, that the desire to exterminate them—like the desire to exterminate rats, poisonous spiders, or wolves—was as natural an instinct as that of self-preservation. (17, 426)

The cruelty of war Tolstoy denounces here in *Hadji Murat* he first offered to the imagination of the reader of 'The Raid' when he mentioned that *kumgan* of milk being thrown to the ground by the laughing Russian raider.

War as it is and the shadow of death in Sevastopol

In the autumn of 1854, Tolstoy, by then a second lieutenant in the Russian Army, was transferred at his request to the Crimean Peninsula, where Russia was at war with England, France, and the Ottoman Empire. His Sevastopol tales—'Sevastopol in December', 'Sevastopol in May', and 'Sevastopol in August, 1855'—were based on his experiences there. The war arose from conflict over religious matters. Russia wanted to protect the rights of Orthodox Christians in the Ottoman Empire and also wanted control over holy sites in Palestine. But this Crimean War of 1853–6 was ultimately a struggle for control over a strategically important area.

It is often called the first modern war: new developments in technology, transportation, and communication were all applied to waging war. It is also the first war that was brought immediately home to the public through photography and through news delivered by telegraph. This meant that the public reacted and responded while the war was still going on.

On the English side, William Russell wrote dispatches for the London *Times* and was, as he put it, 'honoured by a great deal of abuse for telling the truth'. Roger Fenton captured the feel of war in photographic form in his 'Valley of the Shadow of Death', a (possibly staged) photograph of cannonballs on a desolate landscape. Back in England, the poet Tennyson responded in 'The Charge of the Light Brigade', describing how 600 men, following orders, rode into 'the valley of the shadow of death': 'Theirs not to make reply, | Theirs not to reason why, | Theirs but to do and die.' And Florence Nightingale drew attention to the sufferings of the wounded and deaths from infectious diseases that could have been kept in check. With his Sevastopol tales, Tolstoy became part of this modern mode of reporting on war, of bearing witness to suffering in real time, and of prompting the public to reckon with what was being done in their name.

'Sevastopol in December' makes readers into war tourists, and shows us what the narrator of 'The Raid' had wanted to see: 'how people get killed'. Throughout, Tolstoy narrates in the second person, telling 'you' what you see, smell, think, and feel as he takes you through the besieged city to the bastions, where a Russian officer, for *your* entertainment, orders his men to fire on the enemy. Before long, a Russian sailor, wounded in the ensuing skirmish, utters his dying words from a stretcher: 'farewell, forgive me, brothers' (95). Tolstoy pays respect to 'the plain untheatrical hero' often ignored in war stories. While the story celebrates the brotherly love expressed in this man's last words, it leaves unanswered: why did this man die? Tolstoy's war stories leave the reader to ponder these questions about war.

In the first tale, 'Sevastopol in December', Tolstoy announces to his reader his new, more truthful approach to war: 'you will see war not in its correct, beautiful, and glittering ranks, with music and beating drums, with waving banners and generals prancing on horseback; rather, you will see war as it really is—in blood, in suffering, in death...' (87). For Tolstoy, war 'as it really is' is to be found first and foremost in the hospital, in the amputation room. (Before long, the American poet Walt Whitman, who like Tolstoy wanted to write about what he called 'the real war', would also focus on the hospitals, arguing that it was in the hospitals that the 'marrow of the tragedy' of the US Civil War 'was concentrated'.)

'Sevastopol in December', before taking the reader to the infamous Fourth Bastion where the 'action' is, lingers in the hospital where, again in the second person, 'you' the reader, humbled by the suffering you witness, attempt to make conversation, aware of the inadequacy of what you might say to those who recover from the amputation of an arm or a leg. Finally, you enter the amputation room itself and witness the operation:

> Now, if your nerves are strong, go in at the door to the left; it is there they bandage and operate. There you will see doctors with pale, gloomy faces, and arms red with blood up to the elbows, busy at a bed on which a wounded man lies under chloroform. The doctors are engaged in the horrible but beneficent work of amputation. You will see the sharp curved knife enter the healthy white flesh; you will see the wounded man come back to life with terrible, heart-rending screams and curses. You will see the doctor's assistant toss the amputated arm into a corner and in the same room you will see another wounded man on a stretcher watching the operation, and writhing and groaning not so much from physical pain as from the mental torture of anticipation. You will see ghastly sights that will rend your soul.   (87)

Tolstoy wanted this blunt description to affect the soul of his reader, and he magnified this effect by placing the reader in the role of observer.

Imitation of, and war against, Napoleon in *War and Peace*

War and Peace chronicles the Russian triumph over Napoleon and all he represented in the Russian imagination. Tolstoy's Napoleon is eventually defeated by the Russian winter and the Russian expanses; Moscow empties out and burns, thus disappointing Napoleon's hopes of taking over the city in style.

As *War and Peace* opens in 1805, various young men, including Andrei Bolkonsky, Anatole Kuragin, and Nikolai Rostov, are eager to head off to the Austrian front, where Russians would fight Napoleon. But what are they fighting for? Had the novel opened in 1812, when Napoleon invaded Russian soil, they would have been fighting to defend the motherland. But in 1805, other factors are at play: ambition, boredom, devotion to the tsar. Count Rostov, Nikolai's father, sums them all up, however, when he declares: 'this Buonaparte has turned all their heads; they all think of how he rose from an ensign and became Emperor' (1.1:9, 44). That Rostov calls him by his Corsican name Buonaparte (rather than the Frenchified Bonaparte or just by the first name Napoleon, as befits an emperor) reminds those listening that Napoleon is an upstart. Nonetheless, the young men are inspired by Napoleon's rapid rise to power, and strive to imitate him even though they're off to fight him.

Admiration of Napoleon is rampant in the aristocratic circles Tolstoy depicts, despite the fact that in the first paragraph of the novel Napoleon is declared to be 'the antichrist'. (A salon hostess declares this—in French—for effect.) Pierre Bezukhov admires Napoleon because he believes that Napoleon preserved the ideals of the French Revolution such as 'the rights of man, emancipation from prejudices, and equality of citizenship' (1.1:4, 21). Bolkonsky's pregnant wife Liza counters that atrocities committed at

Napoleon's behest, such as the summary execution of 4,000 prisoners in Jaffa (modern-day Israel), undercut all this (1.1:4, 22).

Bolkonsky has his own reasons for idolizing Napoleon: he had let nothing keep him from achieving his goals. Bolkonsky adapts this to his own situation—in which he feels tied down, 'like a chained convict', to his pregnant wife—and concludes that he should be more like Napoleon, let nothing hold him back, and go to seek glory (1.1:6, 31). Tolstoy imparts to Bolkonsky physical characteristics, such as small hands, to signal his affinity with Napoleon (see Chapter 7, 'Tolstoyan realism').

As Franco Moretti observed, 'literary history would have been very different without Napoleon'. Novels thrive on mobility, ambition, drive, and desire. Napoleon seemed to embody (and encourage in others) all those principles. Napoleon himself was aware of the novelistic arc of his life, remarking, 'What a novel my life is!' Imitation of Napoleon was characteristic of 19th-century French novels like Stendhal's *The Red and the Black*, whose protagonist models his own quest for power on Napoleon's. Like other Russian writers of the time, Tolstoy drew narrative inspiration from the man who the philosopher Hegel had declared the 'soul of the world'—but with the goal being to put Napoleon in his place.

War and Peace debunks myths of military might and theories about great men, showing that history unfolds not according to the plans of officers or Napoleon or Tsar Alexander:

> it was not Napoleon who directed the course of the battle, for none of his orders were executed and during the battle he did not know what was going on before him. So the way in which these people killed one another was not decided by Napoleon's will but occurred independently of him, in accord with the will of hundreds of thousands of people who took part in the common action. It *only seemed* to Napoleon that it all took place by his will.
>
> (3.2:28, 842; emphasis in original)

Rather battles, like the rest of life, unfold according to incremental and cumulative activity that is beyond an individual's control and defies human understanding.

How to tell a true war story

Tolstoy also drew attention to how accounts of battles—oral reports of the participants, their letters home, and their written recollections—deviate from what 'really' happened. As Tolstoy had already observed in 'Sevastopol in December', you can tell that a war story has diverged from the truth if it makes the teller's part 'too important'—that is, if he claims to have acted deliberately, with agency. In contrast, Tolstoy drew attention to the larger forces at play—in culture, in institutions, and possibly even bred in the bone or healthy for the psyche—that required narratives to make sense and be coherent. Tolstoy's mission was to indicate how what 'really' happens at war (and even at home) deviates from neat and purposeful plots.

When in *War and Peace* Nikolai Rostov reports to childhood friends how he was wounded at the Battle of Schöngrabern, he tells the story 'just as those who have taken part in a battle generally do describe it, that is, as they would like it to have been, as they have heard it described by others, and as sounds well, but not at all as it really was'. Tolstoy observes that 'It is very difficult to tell the truth, and young people are rarely capable of it.' Had Rostov told the truth, his friends would have thought ill of him: 'His hearers expected a story of how beside himself and all aflame with excitement, he had flown like a storm at the square, cut his way in, slashed right and left, how his sabre had tasted flesh, and he had fallen exhausted, and so on' (1.3:7, 257–8).

At this point in the novel, the reader has already witnessed what really happened. As Rostov, wounded, approaches the line between friend and foe (and between life and death), he encounters a French soldier, but does not register him as such.

He just sees him as someone who could possibly help him. He can't even imagine that some enemy might want to kill him. In this zone, all are brothers, full of love. Rostov dissolves into questions: 'Who are they? Why are they running? Can they be coming at me? And why? To kill me? *Me* who everybody loves?' (1.2:19, 201). As he faces possible death on the battlefield, Nikolai sheds his role as officer in the Russian army and restores in himself the love for all people that Tolstoy (and his fellow Ant Brothers) believed was worth striving for.

If even the sincere Rostov 'falls into the falsehood' of a coherent narrative, he may be succumbing to the way of the world he lives in. He may be protecting himself from a truth that (as Tolstoy had put it in 'Sevastopol in May') lies buried in the soul of every person and is best left buried, lest this truth make it impossible to go about business as usual. The novel offers a host of reasons why Nikolai might want to avoid this truth: desire to save face, ambition, compulsion to carry on, recognition that the truth about war might be too much to bear. So Rostov tells the tales that make the world go round. However, by presenting readers with 'reality', *War and Peace* leaves it to us to reckon with the abyss between the tales told and what really happened.

The onset of moral nausea

Through his portrayal of Rostov, Tolstoy sharply critiques the nationalism and patriotism that drive wartime narratives of duty, sacrifice, and demonization of the enemy. Rostov, despite taking so naturally to military life and feeling in love with the tsar, eventually grows disillusioned with both war and tsar. Here again Tolstoy uses a military hospital to show 'war in its real expression' both to his reader and to Rostov. At this point, Rostov is seasoned in battle, but, somehow, he has not been prepared for the suffering, squalor, and debilitation he witnesses in the military hospital where he visits his injured squadron commander. This, combined with his disappointment in the tsar (who is cosying up to Napoleon during the peace at Tilsit in 1807), threatens to undo Rostov. The whole social order, the system of army, empire, society, at the head of which is the tsar, starts to unravel in his mind. Yet, he holds it together and soldiers on.

Doubts and disillusionment set in once again for Rostov in 1812, when he exuberantly leads his squadron in a charge against French dragoons, in the process striking a French officer with his sabre and taking him prisoner. But, once he sees the dimple on the other man's chin, it strikes him that it was 'not an enemy's face'. And Rostov feels shame and remorse at having struck him and having nearly killed him. All this shows that even Rostov, patriot that he seemed to be, has in him the seeds of a Tolstoyan brotherly love that transcends and renders absurd distinctions based on nationality.

Tolstoy identifies Rostov's distress as a form of 'moral nausea' (3.1:15, 702). 'Moral nausea' is what Tolstoyan heroes experience when the moral law within tells them that the way of the world—what it practises, what it values, and what it rewards—is wrong, but they persist in just going along with it, remaining complicit, instead of somehow taking action to change what they do or at least speak the truth. Nekhlyudov, the hero of Tolstoy's late novel *Resurrection*, will also be overwhelmed by 'moral nausea'. In *The Kingdom of God Is Within You*, Tolstoy admitted that changing one's way of life is hard to do and that few have the strength to take radical steps. But he always advised 'purify[ing] oneself from falsehood' and 'confess[ing] the truth' and trusting that this will bring about some change. Rostov is starting to do that, even if he, like so many others, does not renounce his way of life.

Pacifism in *War and Peace* and beyond

In *War and Peace*, Tolstoy philosophizes about whether war is necessary and seems to present it as evil but inevitable. He also shows that when Napoleon threatens Russian soil, the 'latent heat of patriotism' takes hold of the Russian soldiers and wins the Battle of Borodino for the Russians (3.2:25, 831). On the eve of the Battle of Borodino, Tolstoy stages one last dialogue about war between Pierre, who was seen early in the novel dreaming of a time when there would be no more war, and Andrei, who responds: 'that will never happen.' At that point, Andrei had also allowed that if wars were only fought out of conviction, then there would be no wars.

But now Andrei is set to fight to defend his home, his father, his sister, and his son. Andrei also argues that it is impossible to wage war according to rules. To pretend that war should or does follow those conventions is like 'a lady who faints when she sees a calf being killed: she is so kind-hearted that she can't look at blood, but enjoys eating the calf served up with sauce'. Andrei's principle is 'Take no prisoners, but kill and be killed' (3.2:25, 231). Has Andrei in fact changed his tune? Or is the 'patriotism' and the defence of his home, his father, his son, and his sister not, ultimately, what drives him on the battlefield the next day? Tolstoy leaves that question open.

Later, when the threat to the motherland seems to have passed, the novel shows moments of brotherly love between Russians and the enemy French, such as Nikolai's younger brother Petya with the French drummer boy prisoner, or some peasant soldiers who take pity on two Frenchmen who have separated themselves from the retreat of Napoleon's army to ask for food: 'they are men, too,' conclude the Russians. Here Tolstoy again shows the potential for brotherhood: individuals act according to a moral law within, while the stars above seem to cheer them on.

But what of the protests against war heard earlier? Have they been erased? Early on, Andrei's sister Marya writes in French in a letter of 'witnessing a heartrending scene' of conscripted serf soldiers being taken off: 'You should have seen the state of the mothers, wives, and children, of the men who were going, and

27

should have heard the sobs. It seems as though mankind has forgotten the laws of its divine Saviour, Who preached love and forgiveness of injuries—whereas men attribute the greatest merit to the skill in the art of killing each other [l'art de s'entretuer]' (1.1:22, 100). In the period after he finished *Anna Karenina*, Tolstoy would embrace Marya's conviction that war, or any form of violence, contradicts Jesus's teachings of love (see Chapter 5, 'Non-violence in Gethsemane, at Yasnaya Polyana, and beyond').

Tolstoy also even eventually shared Pierre's dream of a time when there would be no more wars. And all the chaffing responses, from those who regarded his pacifism as an impossible naive dream, were already familiar to him. Tolstoy had rehearsed them all in *War and Peace* and elsewhere. Thus, when Pierre had expressed his hope of a time when there would be no more war, crotchety old Prince Bolkonsky, Andrei and Marya's father, quipped, 'drain the blood from men's veins and put in water instead, then there will be no more war...' (2.2:14, 422).

In his last war story, *Hadji Murat*, written when Tolstoy was actively promoting pacifism (published after his death), Tolstoy returned to the methods of his earlier war stories. Tolstoy shows the tangled skein of good and evil in the character Hadji Murat and in others. (Hadji Murat was an Avar leader who, after fighting the Russian conquest of the Caucasus, came into conflict with Shamil, the main leader of the resistance, surrendered to the Russians, but then was killed when he tried to escape to free his family.) Everyone in *Hadji Murat* accepts war as a way of life. Everyone has blood on their hands. This includes Tolstoy. He reminds us of this in a symbolic way when, in the prologue, he describes how, walking in the fields back home as an older man, he had bloodied his hands pulling a thistle, in an act that, later, flashing on his inward eye, reminded him of the destructive nature of humankind in general and of the last days and death of Hadji Murat. (He explains that to produce *Hadji Murat* he combined what he imagined, what he gleaned from accounts, and what he remembered from having been in the Caucasus at the time.)

But, toward the end of the work, a feminine voice echoes Tolstoy's initial comment on the destructive nature of humankind. When the Russian soldiers parade around carrying the severed head of Hadji Murat—which retains its distinctive 'childlike' and 'kindly' expression—Marya Dmitrievna, who cooks and cares for the warriors, declares them all to be 'cutthroats'. Though one of the young officers responds by reminding her that 'War's war', Marya refuses to accept such common wisdom and, by extension, rejects all the other adages mustered to justify war, to uphold the existing order, and to make the 'civilized' world go around. Marya's persistence in calling them cut-throats highlights a Tolstoyan truth, even if it's clear that here—as in Sevastopol in May 1854 or in Troy when the *Iliad* ended—the killing will continue.

In his later treatises against war, Tolstoy himself spoke out directly, developing arguments out of the truths that his characters or his narrators let loose in his war stories, starting with 'The Raid'. Thus, in 1904, he wrote a piece called 'Bethink Yourselves', denouncing the recently declared war between Russia and Japan. It appeared in English and was published in both the *New York Times* and London *Times* as well as in pamphlet form. The title derived from the melding of two Gospel passages (in Tolstoy's rendition): 'The time is fulfilled and the Kingdom of God is at hand, bethink yourselves and believe in the Gospel' (Mark 1:15), and 'if you do not bethink yourselves you will all perish' (Luke 13:5). Tolstoy believed that 'the right way to stop war is to stop making war' (in Ernest Crosby's paraphrase). It was time for people to bethink themselves, that is, to engage in intense deliberation and resolve to save themselves from destruction. The same message had already long been present in his war stories.

Chapter 3
Love

Tolstoy's brothers took him to a brothel soon after his fourteenth birthday. After he 'committed the act', he 'stood by the woman's bedside and wept'. From this loss of virginity, through love affairs and marriage, through the birth of over a dozen children, through advocacy of chastity later in life (before the birth of his youngest children), to acrimony between him and his wife that ended in him leaving home right before his death, Tolstoy's love life has been extensively documented and debated. Tolstoy himself addressed all this directly in letters, in diaries, and in frank conversation with memoirists; others involved, including his wife, also left their own accounts.

Tolstoy's major fiction, known for its autobiographical and 'autopsychological' elements, roughly follows the trajectory of Tolstoy's life and loves. Tolstoy begins with the yearnings of the motherless child for love and the myths of happy Russian gentry childhood in *Childhood, Boyhood, Youth*. He celebrates Russian marriage and family life (and tames sexual desire) in *War and Peace*. He then explores adulterous passion, the tender joys of conjugal love, and family unhappiness in *Anna Karenina*. He excoriates sex, marriage, and family life in 'The Kreutzer Sonata'. In his late love fiction, Tolstoy favours quests to expiate sexual guilt or else parables of love and death among simple folk.

In his depictions of loving families and of romantic passion, whether conjugal or adulterous, Tolstoy includes reminders of the call to love God and neighbour, as he, along with his characters, asks whether it's possible somehow to combine, balance, or reconcile these loves. Or do certain forms of love, by their very nature, exclude others? Tolstoy's heroes often have insights that look ahead to Sigmund Freud's questions about loving your neighbour: doesn't it conflict with one's duty to 'one's own people'? Tolstoy himself came to see both sex and family life as service of the self rather than of God. Tolstoyan heroes are often haunted by the Ant Brothers' dream of love and happiness for all. It may be an insurmountable obstacle on their course toward family happiness or sexual bliss.

As Tolstoy put it in his *Confession*, marriage and family life seemed to bring him happiness and give meaning to his life, until he began to regard them, like all worldly activities, as a diversion from what really mattered, which was faith. He needed to find 'meaning in life that inevitable death awaiting [him] would not destroy' (5, 24). Leaving children or *Anna Karenina* behind after death was not a consolation to him. Nor were they enough to divert him any longer. But even fiction written before this realization reveals Tolstoy's anxieties about loving and being loved in the face of death.

Love's challenges in *Childhood, Boyhood, Youth*

Sex, love, and marriage get off to a bad start in Tolstoy's work. The first romantic kisses in his fiction occur when Nikolai Irtenev, the hero of *Childhood, Boyhood, Youth*, three days after his tenth birthday, kisses the shoulder and then the arm of Katya, the daughter of the French governess. In a chapter called 'Grisha', Nikolai ventures the second kiss as the children of the household hide in the dark in order to spy on Grisha the Holy Fool. Although Nikolai is temporarily transfixed by Grisha's love, faith, and devotion to God, he is quickly drawn back into the fun and games of his peers and, when jostled by Katya, he responds by kissing her arm. This kiss sets a pattern for Nikolai and perhaps for some of Tolstoy's later heroes: they bumble through courtship even as they are fascinated by religious feeling that seems to transcend romantic love.

At the same time, *Childhood, Boyhood, Youth* presents a bleak picture of marriage, starting with Nikolai's parents' marriage. Nikolai's father is reported to have had 'affairs with countless women' (10, 36). Nikolai's beloved mother bears it meekly until her death. By the end of *Youth* his father has got remarried to a woman who wanders through the house at night, unkempt, eating cold veal or a pickle from the pantry, and waiting for her husband, who she believes to be unfaithful to her, to come home.

Tucked into *Childhood* are two forerunners of heroes of Tolstoy's later work who seek meaning in life beyond sex and marriage: Grisha the Holy Fool and Natalya Savishna. Unlike most other men around, Grisha does not live for sex and success. And Nikolai has witnessed in him a love, devotion, ecstasy, and faith that are unlike anything else he experiences in childhood, boyhood, or youth. Another force of love in *Childhood* is his mother's serf, Natalya Savishna, who had been forbidden to marry her sweetheart in her youth and thereafter selflessly devoted herself to loving God and to caring for Nikolai's mother and her children. As Tolstoy writes it, the impression these two made on Nikolai as a child helps explain why believing in happy romantic love is a challenge.

Courtship, marriage, and family happiness in *War and Peace*

Tolstoy worked on *War and Peace* from 1863 to 1869 during what is generally thought to have been a relatively happy time in his family life: in 1862, at 34, he married Sophia Behrs, the 18-year-old daughter of a childhood friend. Although the diaries and letters of both husband and wife reveal tensions from the wedding night on, Tolstoy considered himself a happy man when first married. It was in this state that he wrote *War and Peace*.

Tolstoy toyed with the idea of calling the novel *All's Well That Ends Well* and having it, in what he saw as typical of English novels, depend on marriages 'to unravel the knots of the plot'. As *War and Peace* swings into action in a St Petersburg salon, Tolstoy shows that courtship, marriage, and family life in the more Westernized imperial capital lack soul. Flirtation is illicit and matchmaking is crass. In contrast, when Tolstoy shifts the action to the Rostov household in Moscow, the mother of Russian cities, Tolstoy shows a gentry family in action, as they celebrate the name day of mother and daughter, both named Natalya. The young folk frolic, exchange kisses, and shed tears. And everyone, young and old, kin and outsider, male and female, master and serf, gathers to watch with delight as Count Rostov dances energetically with Natasha's godmother known as 'the terrible dragon'. All that Tolstoy presents here shows this Russian family as a life force ready to take on Napoleon and the system that he represents (see Box 1).

At the end of *War and Peace* in 1821, most surviving members of the younger generation have married. Tolstoy scrambled all the couples that were starting to form in 1805 as the novel opened. One exception is Berg and Vera, the eldest of the Rostov children and an outlier in her own family: this couple achieves bourgeois happiness early in *War and Peace*. Natasha moves through a series of suitors, and finally is seen fruitfully married to Pierre Bezukhov, with whom she'd danced in the opening scene. And Nikolai Rostov, absolved in a most opportune way of his promise to marry the dowerless Sonya, a cousin who grew up among the Rostovs, has married the wealthy Marya Bolkonskaya.

The brilliance of this Russian 'all's well that ends well' ending is that Tolstoy keeps it from feeling triumphant, pat, or even that

Box 1 Russian names

As readers land at the Rostovs' party, they find that there is a host of characters to keep track of and that a given character may be referred to by a variety of forms of his or her name. This makes it harder to keep track of who's who. Most translations of Tolstoy's novels list the characters and the various names used for each of them. But it helps to get a feel for how these names work.

Russian names have three components: first name, patronymic, and surname or family name. The first name is chosen at birth from a fairly limited repertory of names. And names repeat in families, as illustrated by the fact that both mother and daughter are named Natalya (which happens to have a root meaning birth!).

Nicknames or diminutives are formed from first names. Thus, the daughter—and heroine of *War and Peace*—is often called Natasha. French versions of first names are used in certain contexts and for some characters, like Pierre Bezukhov, more than others.

The second name or patronymic is formed by adding a suffix to the father's first name. The younger Natalya's patronymic is Ilyinichna, which designates her as the daughter of Ilya; her brother Nikolai's patronymic is the masculine form, which is Ilyich. The patronymic is used in combination with the first name as a formal form of address.

Children inherit the surname of their father; for most names there will be a feminine form, such as Rostova, and a masculine form, Rostov. (The Russian root of this last name means 'growth', which, combined with Natalya, adds to the aura of fertility.)

Some of the families in *War and Peace* also have inherited titles such as Count and Countess or Prince and Princess: when these are used, they draw attention to social status.

much like an ending. For example, the love that develops between
Natasha and Pierre, which first floods his heart as he witnesses
the comet of 1812, has an aura not so much of being fated as of
being the natural reward for their suffering during the war and for
their past sexual travails. Natasha and Pierre emerge as if purified,
no longer bearing the taint of the oversexed Kuragin family, with
which each had earlier become entangled. To make this happy
ending possible, the Kuragin siblings are done away with. Anatole
Kuragin, who destroyed Natasha's reputation, is last seen getting
his leg amputated in a field station after the Battle of Borodino;
Hélène Kuragina, Pierre's first wife, is dead, in circumstances
suggesting a botched abortion. Natasha, in contrast, is presented
as the apotheosis of motherhood at the end of the novel.

In his portrait of the marriage of Natasha and Pierre, Tolstoy
shows on the one hand a very traditional apportioning of gender
roles, with Natasha caring only about her family and Pierre
concerned with the welfare of others. As her brother notes after
an argument, Natasha has 'no words of her own' and just
repeats what Pierre says. Yet Tolstoy also suggests that it's hard to
tell in the relations of husband and wife who is the master and
who is the slave. He especially praises their mystic mode of
understanding and communicating with each other when they
are alone (Epilogue 1:16, 1265).

But all's not entirely well in the epilogue of *War and Peace*. Happy
as he is as husband and father, Pierre does not devote himself
only to loving those near and dear. He has just returned from

Petersburg where he has become involved in political action for the common welfare. Tolstoy envisioned Pierre as taking part in what culminated in the Decembrist Revolt of 1825 and led to the execution of some participants and exile to Siberia for others. Pierre likens what he and others are involved in to other liberal movements across Europe that were inspired by 'love' and 'mutual help' and 'what Christ preached from the Cross' (Epilogue 1:14, 1259). As *War and Peace* ends, Pierre seems unable to ignore the plight of others beyond his family circle. And this poses a threat to family happiness.

Tolstoy shows Marya, who had in her maiden years fantasized about running away from her family to become a pilgrim, one of the 'God's folk', seemingly content as wife and mother (2.3:26, 520–1). In the final scene between husband and wife, Nikolai complains of all Pierre's talk about 'love of neighbor and Christianity', and justifies his focus on his own affairs, his family, and serfs. For her part, Marya, ever spiritual, affirms their God-given duties to their nearest neighbours, that is, their own children, but she also chides herself for loving her own children more than her nephew and ward, Nikolai Bolkonsky, whose parents Andrei and Liza are both dead. We're told that her soul 'always strove towards the infinite, the eternal, and the absolute, and could therefore never be at peace' (Epilogue 1:15, 1264).

Tolstoy posits in Marya, a character thought to be a fictional incarnation of the mother he never knew, a sense of religious responsibility for others beyond her maternal embrace. She cannot be at peace while others sorrow. And thus she strives to love *all* 'as Christ loved mankind' (Epilogue 1:16, 1264). On her final appearance in *War and Peace*, 'A stern expression of the lofty, secret suffering of a soul burdened by the body appeared on her face.' This leaves her husband thinking, 'O God! What will become of us if she dies, as I always fear when her face is like that?' Even if Sonya, Nikolai's former sweetheart, appears to be ready to take Marya's place, this foreshadowing of Marya's death, which will leave her children motherless, reminds us of Tolstoy's anxiety about the transitory nature of family happiness.

Adultery and marriage in *Anna Karenina*

While the famous opening sentence of *Anna Karenina* claims happy and unhappy families are fundamentally different, both the successful and failed marriages in the novel explore fundamental questions about love such as: is family happiness possible? And can sex ever lead to happiness?

Dolly Oblonskaya meditates on the pursuit of happiness as she rides through the Russian countryside from Levin's estate, where she and her children have been spending the summer, to visit Anna Karenina, now living on her lover Vronsky's estate with their baby daughter. Dolly, who Anna convinced at the opening of the novel to stay with her philandering husband (and Anna's brother) Stiva, now starts asking herself whether motherhood is worth the labour, anxiety, and pain (6:16, 609–11). Without her children in this moment, she feels as though she has just been 'released from prison'. She even muses about having an affair of her own. 'God has put into our hearts' the desire 'to live', so how can she, Dolly, condemn Anna for seeking happiness with Vronsky? But when Dolly then sees Anna apparently consumed by sexual love, practising birth control, and ignoring her young daughter, Dolly recoils from her and, happy or not, wants to be back with her children.

As many readers have noted, Tolstoy turns the sympathetic Anna of the opening of the novel into a sex fiend and then 'throws her under the train'. He thus follows the pattern of novels of adultery like Flaubert's *Madame Bovary* that condemn the adulteress to death. But what distinguishes Anna Karenina from Emma Bovary—and *Anna Karenina* from *Madame Bovary*—is that, as Matthew Arnold noted, Tolstoy gives Anna 'treasures of compassion, tenderness, insight' Flaubert's Emma lacks.

Flaubert treats Emma with cruelty and irony even on her deathbed: as the priest performs the last rites, Emma catches sight of a crucifix and, 'fastening her lips to the body of the Man-God, bestowed upon it with every ounce of her dying strength the most passionate kiss she had ever given'. By contrast, those 'treasures of compassion, tenderness, and insight' come out in Anna when, in her despair, she is ready to throw herself under a train, rids herself of her red handbag, remembers her maidenly self, makes the sign of the cross, begs God for forgiveness, and attempts to save herself, too late, as the train is upon her. Whereas Flaubert exaggerates Emma's response with that 'most passionate kiss' to 'the body of the Man-God', Tolstoy makes Anna's remorse of a different order as she begs, 'Lord, forgive me for everything' (7.31, 771).

Tolstoy juxtaposes the adulterous passion of Anna and Vronsky with the conjugal love of Kitty and Levin, a love that stands out in Tolstoy's fiction for its apparent purity. However, Tolstoy also uses their relationship to think through his own questions, such as whether love and intimacy between two people is really possible and whether people on this earth are only ever alone. While the first proposal ends in refusal, during the second proposal scene Levin and Kitty share telepathic powers of communication as they divine each other's meaning from merely spelling out the initial letters of the intended words. This suggests a mystical bond.

Yet, when Levin, in his joy, looks at Kitty during the marriage ceremony, wonders what she's thinking, and concludes that she's feeling what he's feeling, Tolstoy states plainly that Levin is wrong (5:4, 455). Levin doesn't in fact know Kitty's mind. For all their mutual love at this point, Tolstoy thus calls attention to the gulf that separates them. Even the purity of Kitty and Levin's romantic love does not protect them from the loneliness that haunts Tolstoy's heroes (Figure 3).

Tolstoy incorporates into this wedding scene other perspectives on love and marriage. Some women bystanders at the church

3. Kitty and Levin at their wedding in *Anna Karenina*, illustration by Yuri Pimenov.

admire the bride but say she is 'like a lamb dressed for slaughter!' And they add that they feel sorry for their 'sister', whatever anyone might say (5:5, 459). Meanwhile, the sight of Kitty during the ceremony reminds her sister Dolly not only of her own past 'love, hope, and fear' under those solemn circumstances, but also of the love, hope, and fear 'of all women' and, in particular, she remembers 'her dear Anna' and how 'she too had stood there just

as purely, adorned with orange blossoms and a veil. And now?'
Dolly thinks to herself. Tolstoy undercuts the joy.

Witnessing the death of his brother Nikolai, which occurs at the
end of his honeymoon, Levin feels 'the need for life and for love in
spite of death' because of the nearness of his wife (5:20, 507). She is
confirmed to be pregnant by the same doctor who cared for his
dying brother. During Kitty's pregnancy, Levin experiences 'the
radiant pleasure, still novel to him, of an intimacy with the woman
that he loved which was completely free of sensuality' (6:3, 560).
Tolstoy suggests that theirs may be the purest love this side of Eden.

Yet, a couple of chapters later, Levin is overwhelmed by jealousy
when a visitor, Kitty's male cousin twice removed, appears to be
flirting with her. After tense and tearful scenes, with Kitty at one
point 'rejoicing in the depths of her soul at the intensity of his love
for her, which was now being expressed in his jealousy', husband
and wife make up (6:7, 576). Levin banishes Kitty's cousin from
the estate. The couple appears to settle into family happiness,
until, in Moscow for the birth of their child, Levin for the first
time meets Anna, who is living with Vronsky while still married
to Karenin. When Levin gets home, Kitty is convinced that Anna,
'that nasty woman', has 'bewitched' her husband because she can
see it in his eyes (7:11, 705). This crisis is immediately followed
by Kitty giving birth. Levin experiences fatherhood only as 'a
consciousness of a new area of vulnerability' (7:16, 721). Love
for his son only comes later, at the end of *Anna Karenina*.

But, precious as it is, this family love is not enough to sustain
Levin. When even Levin, a loving husband, finds himself unable
to carry on, *Anna Karenina* illustrates the truth that Tolstoy
reveals directly in his *Confession*: that marriage and family life
were a diversion from the grim reality of death, from seeking the
meaning of life, and from his quest for God. On the last day of
Anna Karenina, Levin moves from despair and doubt to affirming
that he can endow his life with meaning and goodness. And yet in

the same final words Levin acknowledges that 'there will still be the same wall between the holy of holies of my soul and other people, even my wife' (8:19, 821). Thus, for Levin, and for Anna, whose circumstances were so different, Tolstoy ends the novel by affirming a sense of them standing alone before God, with spiritual yearnings that sex and family love do not satisfy.

Sex as scandal in 'The Kreutzer Sonata'

In Tolstoy's novella 'The Kreutzer Sonata' (1889), Pozdnyshev murders his wife in a fit of jealousy, suspecting her of committing adultery with the violinist with whom she plays Beethoven's sonata. As Pozdnyshev explains, Beethoven's music is somehow to blame: it works those who perform it—and those who listen to it—into a frenzy and amounts to what Tolstoy would later label 'bad art'. But Pozdnyshev's confession to a murder committed under the influence of Beethoven's music turns into a harangue against sex as he seeks to explain away his murder by attributing it to the sex-ridden environment in which he, his wife, and others of their class lived.

All this frank talk about sex in and out of marriage scandalized many, starting with various authorities, from Russian censors, who initially banned publication, to the US Post Office, which made it illegal to mail it. The tsar eventually interceded to allow it to be published as part of Tolstoy's complete works, and the ban in the USA was eventually lifted. In England, critics of 'The Kreutzer Sonata' averred that Tolstoy might have been less categorical in condemning sex had he had an 'idea of that noble Anglo-Saxon type of love in which...soul and body blend in one full chord to form the marriage tie'.

'The Kreutzer Sonata' provoked its Russian readers too and prompted soul-searching and debate about sexual mores. For example, Chekhov, though he criticized its portrayal of female sexuality, found it 'extremely thought-provoking': 'As I read it

I could hardly keep myself from exclaiming, "That's true!" or "That's ridiculous!"' In Boris Pasternak's *Doctor Zhivago* (1957), 'The Kreutzer Sonata' would be important to the sentimental education of Zhivago and his friends as they came of age in the early 1900s and partly responsible for them developing a 'mania for preaching chastity'. Reading Tolstoy made them look at romantic love in their society in a new, guilt-ridden light.

The sexual marketplace and family strife

Pozdnyshev presents his sexual past—until the murder—as typical of men of his milieu. He was just doing what everyone around him not only condoned, but considered necessary. Pozdnyshev's account has features in common with Tolstoy's own sex life and with Levin's in *Anna Karenina*. Pozdnyshev lost his virginity to a prostitute under peer pressure, and then went through a period of debauchery in which he engaged in sexual relations with women without any moral responsibility. And Pozdnyshev, like Tolstoy and Levin, recorded his sexual transgressions in a diary that he gave to his bride before the wedding.

In his monologue, Pozdnyshev carries to their logical—or absurd—conclusion the insights into courtship, sex, marriage, and family life that Tolstoy had only hinted at in earlier works. Pozdnyshev rails against the practice in which mothers initiate their daughters by dressing them in a sexualized, seductive way. He claims he never would have fallen for his wife had she not been wearing a tight-fitting jersey when they went out boating in the moonlight. Pozdnyshev's comments cast a cynical light on the scene in *War and Peace* when Natasha Rostova, stifling her innate sense of shame, appears in a ball gown, with her neck and arms bare for the first time, at the ball in Petersburg. At that ball, Natasha attracts Andrei Bolkonsky, her future fiancé.

Pozdnyshev's view that courtship practices in his milieu amount to a market or bazaar, with all attempts at educating young women aimed simply at catching a husband, harks back to Kitty's experience in *Anna Karenina*. After refusing Levin only to be jilted by Vronsky, Kitty finds her life bereft of meaning, but then rejoices when she finds in her new friend Varenka 'a model of what she was now painfully seeking: interests in life, virtues in life, beyond a girl's relations with men in society, which Kitty found odious, and which for her now resembled the shameful parading of goods awaiting purchasers' (2:30, 219). Nasty as he is, Pozdnyshev simply speaks out loud what Kitty had once felt in her maidenly heart.

Tolstoy wrote an 'Afterword' to 'The Kreutzer Sonata' to explain where he stood on the matters addressed by Pozdnyshev. Tolstoy argued that chastity was the ideal to strive for, even in marriage. And he revealed that he shared many of the views voiced by Pozdnyshev. He too believed that the society he lived in glorified sex, justified debauchery, hoodwinked everyone into believing sex was necessary and desirable. Writers and artists were complicit. Because 'falling in love' was extolled as the highest (and 'most poetic') human endeavour, people wasted so much of their lives on activities that were 'not merely unproductive, but injurious'. Tolstoy argued that romantic love, marriage, and family life limited people's capacity for loving God and neighbour.

Pozdnyshev's view of parenthood is especially bleak. Pozdnyshev reports none of the joy that children sometimes brought to their parents in Tolstoy's earlier fiction. The Pozdnyshev children 'poison' their parents' lives, provide new pretexts for quarrels, and become 'weapons' in their strife. Husband and wife each have 'favourites' and 'allies' among their children and are too involved in their 'incessant warfare' to pay any attention to them for their own sake (16, 125).

Intimations of family unhappiness like the Pozdnyshevs' had lurked in Tolstoy's earlier novels. In the epilogue of *War and Peace*, Nikolai gets annoyed at Marya and their son for waking him up from a nap after they have had a mild tiff, but then he doesn't mind when his favourite daughter, 'her father's pet', comes in and climbs on him (Epilogue 1:9, 1240). In *Anna Karenina*, which opens with the quarrel between Dolly and Stiva over his adultery with the children's governess, Stiva is shown offering chocolates to his daughter Tanya, identified as his 'favorite', but Tanya immediately asks if one piece is for her brother, as if in an attempt to undo her father's unfairness and favouritism (1:3, 10). The fact that seemingly happy families are subject to mild forms of the discord described by Pozdnyshev makes his tale all the more disturbing. What will keep it from escalating?

Overcoming passion

Pozdnyshev's tale of how he murdered his wife is not so much a confession, as an indictment of the sexualized world he lives in, a world in which others are guilty of the sexual sins if not the capital crime he commits. But at one point he does seem to understand the gravity of his act. As his wife lay dying after he had stabbed her with a Damascus dagger, he was taken to her bedside, while their children stood in the doorway. Looking at her 'bruised, disfigured face... for the first time I forgot myself, my rights, my pride, and for the first time saw the human being in her' (28, 161). In this way, Pozdnyshev acknowledges that he had objectified her. So sex-crazed was he that he never saw her as a person in her own right. In drafts of this scene, Tolstoy had Pozdnyshev say: 'I saw a sister in her.' While the term sister was not necessarily meant here in a literal way, at other points in his advocacy of chastity, Tolstoy would return to this motif of regarding each and every woman as a sister. Would someone want to subject his own sister to such vile acts?

Here Pozdnyshev also goes through a sequence that is familiar from other (less extreme) characters in Tolstoy's fiction for whom it is only when the proximity of death (and/or birth) brings sexuality to naught that men and women see each other as human beings. Thus, Anna Karenina, suffering from an infection to her womb after the birth of her lovechild, draws Karenin and Vronsky together in love and forgiveness. As she recovers, desire returns, along with jealousy and enmity and egoism, but for this period as death hovers over them, they see each other as human beings and love and forgive each other. (See Chapter 4, 'Memento mori in *Anna Karenina*'.) Similarly, in *War and Peace*, Andrei Bolkonsky, hitherto unable to forgive Anatole Kuragin (his romantic rival, whom he dreamed of killing in a duel), finds himself at the Battle of Borodino lying side by side with Anatole in a hospital station: Andrei is suffering from a wound that will end up being fatal, and Anatole has just had his leg amputated. At this point, Andrei loves and forgives his 'enemy', seeing him as a human being and a brother for the first time.

In Tolstoy's world, sexual passion and sexual jealousy are not easy to overcome. Love and forgiveness do not seem to happen without these severed limbs, stabbed breasts, or infected wombs. In his later stories, this pattern continues, becoming even more graphic: in 'Father Sergius', the hero chops off his finger with an axe in an effort to overcome lust. And 'The Devil' has as its epigraph Matthew 5:28–30 where Jesus says that it is more profitable to sever a member than to have one's whole body go to hell.

From sexual guilt to responsibility and resurrection

When Tolstoy's friend and biographer saw him in the last year of his life, Tolstoy said he didn't want him 'only to write pleasant things', as this would render the account 'untrue and incomplete'. The biographer should 'mention the bad things too'. Among these, two episodes from youth were 'a special torment' to Tolstoy in his old age. These were a liaison with a local peasant woman named Aksinya Bazykina, who gave birth to his son in 1860, as well as a 'crime' against his aunt's parlour-maid: 'she was innocent, I seduced her, she was dismissed and ruined.'

Although Tolstoy used his late fiction to explore his own sexual guilt for past transgressions, in his major novels he touched on the question of masters having sexual relations with female serfs, servants, or peasants only obliquely or incidentally. For example, in *War and Peace*, 'Uncle', a distant cousin of the Rostovs, lives happily with a peasant as his common-law wife. In *Anna Karenina*, Levin muses at one point about marrying a peasant, but then realizes that he loves Kitty.

Sexual guilt for the seduction of a maid is the kernel of Tolstoy's late novel *Resurrection*. Dmitry Nekhlyudov, a Russian gentleman, finds himself on a jury that is to pass judgement on a prostitute accused of poisoning a client. The juror recognizes the prostitute as Katya, a maid he seduced, impregnated, and abandoned in his youth. While trying to make amends to the young woman, Tolstoy's hero is exposed to—and devastated by—the ills of the Russian penal system, from the courts, to the prison convoys, to conditions in Siberia. Just as he thinks he might make amends to Katya, he begins to understand that he bears responsibility for the misery of all the convicts. The whole social order—from bedroom to prison—is rotten, and he has a part in that.

Nekhlyudov now sours on Missy, the young woman everyone expects to become his bride, and finds relations with her 'horrid and shameful'. His sexual shame and horror even infect his feelings for his own dead mother. As he, attempting to restore pleasant memories of her, looks on her portrait, what strikes him is how the artist depicted 'with particular care the outlines of the breasts, the space between them, the dazzlingly beautiful shoulders and the neck', and her 'triumphant smile' (2:28, 329–30).

His disillusionment with the sexual mores of his privileged class continues. At another point, Nekhlyudov notices an uncanny similarity between what occurs between him and a prostitute on the street in Petersburg and what occurs between him and Marie, an old acquaintance, now the wife of an important figure in

Petersburg to whom he was appealing on behalf of a prisoner. Nekhlyudov realized that this Marie, as she smiled at him, was, really, essentially offering herself to him and that 'the only difference' was that the prostitute's body language 'said plainly and openly, "If you want me, take me; if not, go on your way," and the other one pretended that she was not thinking of this, but living in some high and refined state—while the same thing was really at the root' (2:28, 330). With its intense anxiety about sex, *Resurrection* undoes the traditional love novel, as it chronicles disillusionment with the traditional subject matter of novels: romantic love, sex, and family life.

Love, courtship, and marriage among the folk

Writing in his diary in 1884, during a period of intense questioning of his way of life and his writing, Tolstoy reflected on his unsuccessful attempts at writing a novel that featured peasant life and folk ways. He concluded that he had failed because the kind of romantic love that was expected in novels was not part of the peasant experience (49:102–3). Tolstoy, however, found short stories to be a more suitable genre for describing peasant life.

'Alyosha Pot', often considered one of Tolstoy's better stories for and about the folk, puts a twist on the romance plot, peasant-style. The hero of the story, Alyosha, whose life has been a series of hardships that he humbly bears, works as a servant for a merchant while his father pockets his wages. Then one day Alyosha learns that Ustinya, a maid in the household, 'pities' him (151). The attachment grows and the two of them make plans to marry. However, Alyosha's father learns that the master and mistress of the house, who are worried that Ustinya would get pregnant and not do her work, disapprove of them marrying. Alyosha's father forbids the marriage. Alyosha submits to his father's will and ends the courtship. Shortly after, during Lent, Alyosha falls from the roof while clearing snow and, as he lies dying, he thanks Ustinya for her pity and remarks that 'it's better they stopped us marrying, there would have been no point. Everything is all right now' (154). Then he dies.

Unlike a conventional romantic hero, Alyosha submits to the will of his father and the merchant. Tolstoy had no interest in making this into a tragic Romeo-and-Juliet love plot transposed to peasant life. Nor is it an example of a comedic plot in which young lovers triumph over parental constraints or other obstacles. In this story about love among the Russian folk, Tolstoy presents a new kind of hero. Instead of being driven by selfish sexual desire, Alyosha is characterized by his humility, his generosity of spirit, and his compassion. In Tolstoy's fictional world, Alyosha's may be the truest love of all. It may make a disappointing or upsetting (romantic) love story, but Alyosha's last words to his beloved—'everything is all right now'—suggest that, as he sees it, his is a case of 'all's well that ends well'. While this ending might unsettle readers, it reflects the tone of Tolstoy's late stories in which sexual love does not bring happiness.

Throughout much of Tolstoy's fiction, romantic and/or family happiness are what, for better or for worse, most people strive for. (And they may be what his readers read for.) In his early *Childhood, Boyhood, Youth*, his late stories 'The Kreutzer Sonata' and 'Father Sergius', and his last novel *Resurrection*, Tolstoy presents a bleak view of sexual love and marriage. In *War and Peace* and *Anna Karenina*, he celebrates love and marriage, but not without showing just how precarious family happiness is. All along, Tolstoy troubles his love plots. Then, in a story like 'Alyosha Pot', he transcends them. Alyosha recalls Natalya Savishna and Grisha the Holy Fool of 'Childhood'. All three of these folk heroes embody Tolstoy's concern, which intensified as life went on, that that selfless love of others and devotion to God might be the only kinds of love to bring everlasting happiness.

Chapter 4
Death

Tolstoy in the valley of the shadow of death

Death was a fact of Tolstoy's life from early on. His mother died when he was not yet 2—as he put it, 'before [he] could even call her mama' (55:374). His father died suddenly when Tolstoy was not yet 9. As a young man, Tolstoy witnessed and caused death at war. His brother Dmitry died of tuberculosis in 1856 when Tolstoy was in his late twenties; just four years later, Tolstoy was at the deathbed of Nikolai, his oldest brother, the mastermind of the Ant Brothers game. He too died of tuberculosis. While Tolstoy was at work on *Anna Karenina* in the 1870s, two aunts, who had cared for him and his siblings, also died, as did three of Tolstoy's own children. By the time of his own death in 1910, three more of his children had died.

Although he had his own memorable brushes with death—on a raid in Chechnya, on the bastions of Sevastopol, and on a bear hunt—Tolstoy was also subject to bouts of anxiety about death that came over him without physical cause. In 1869, in a hotel room in Arzamas, the presence of death suddenly overwhelmed him. This became the kernel of his story 'Notes of a Madman' (published posthumously). Grim thoughts of death brought him to another crisis as he was finishing *Anna Karenina*. As he reveals in his *Confession*, he became horrified at the thought that nothing would remain of his life but 'stench and worms'. The question that haunted him was: 'Is there any meaning in my life that the inevitable death awaiting me does not destroy...?' (5, 24). Tolstoy addresses his own concern with death and dying as he wrote.

Early in his career, in 'Sevastopol in May', Tolstoy observed that 'the angel of death had been hovering unceasingly' above Sevastopol for months, before describing life in the besieged city under these extreme circumstances (1, 97). But, whether he was writing about a war zone, a pastoral landscape, a slum, or a domestic scene, Tolstoy's works are set in the 'valley of the shadow of death' (Psalm 23:4). One of Tolstoy's missions as a writer was to remind readers of their own mortality and to make them think about how to live and love in the face of death.

Death in *Childhood* and the motherless child

Death and dying were a focus of Tolstoy's fiction from the start. His first published work, *Childhood*, otherwise rather plotless (according to early critics), culminates in the death of the hero's mother. The work opens with 10-year-old Nikolai Irtenev fabricating a dream about his mother's death. Asked why he is crying and not wanting to admit the petty cause of his tears, Nikolai claims to have dreamt that his beloved mother had died. In a flashback to seemingly happier days, when he was a toddler, drinking sweet milk in his high chair, alone with his mother, she asks him whether he will still remember her when she is dead. On some level, she herself had been planting the seeds of his invented but prophetic dream. Far from being happy-go-lucky, his childhood has been lived in the shadow of death.

The holy fool Grisha, featured in two chapters of *Childhood*, is a living reminder of mortality and death. Nikolai's mother welcomes him into their home and recalls that a holy fool had prophesied the death of her own father. Grisha babbles about 'dear ones fly[ing] away', which conjures up not only young ones leaving the nest, but also the departure of the soul from the body at death (5, 21). And Grisha wears chains to remind himself (and all who hear them clang) of mortality.

At his mother's funeral, Nikolai observes everyone around him. The first-person narration captures the point of view of this child apprehending death for the first time. He describes how the grown-ups at the funeral rush to call him an orphan, how the priest prays in a rote fashion, and how his father grieves histrionically. But these labels, rituals, and conventions—which Tolstoy believed society resorted to in order to shield everyone from death—are meaningless to this motherless child. Nothing seems authentic until a young peasant girl, brought to pay her last respects, is overwhelmed by the sight and smell of the corpse. She screams and Nikolai joins her. The children's spontaneous sincerity shows up the adults' attempts to civilize death.

Nikolai's mother's death at the end of *Childhood* haunts the sequels *Boyhood* and *Youth*. Even as Nikolai attempts to follow in his father's and older brother's footsteps and adapt to the norms of masculine behaviour and succeed, he continues to struggle with his mother's absence and legacy and to view himself as a motherless child.

Nikolai is the first in a long line of Tolstoyan heroes who lose their mothers in childhood or youth: Pierre as well as Andrei and Marya (*War and Peace*); Levin and his brothers, as well as Anna and Stiva (*Anna Karenina*). Even the piebald gelding, whose equine consciousness Tolstoy enters in his story 'Strider' (1886), suffers from the loss of his mother. As a result of their loss, these motherless heroes often have trouble conforming to the way of the world or are spiritually restless.

Death on the front and at home
in *War and Peace*

In *War and Peace*, Tolstoy presents not only death (and near death) on the battlefield, death by firing squad, death at the hands of a mob incited by a political leader, death in a military hospital, but also death at childbirth, death from a botched abortion, and death of old age. He shows men fighting a duel which, had it resulted in death, would have been 'murder' (2.1:4, 336). Tolstoy's message in *War and Peace* in regard to death is encapsulated in the early scene at the Rostovs' name day celebration. When Count Rostov affirms that his son Nikolai is going off to war, one of his visitors counters that she has four sons in the army and does not fret: 'It is all in the hands of the Lord. You may die in your bed or God may spare you in battle' (1.1:16, 68).

In *War and Peace*, Tolstoy brings Andrei Bolkonsky close to death at the Battle of Austerlitz. (He had originally planned on killing him off there, but changed his mind.) As he lies wounded, Andrei sees all that preoccupied him before as vanity of vanities. When, by coincidence, Napoleon himself inspects the casualties and declares Andrei to be *'une belle mort'* [a fine death], Andrei dismisses his former hero Napoleon as insignificant. To him, Napoleon is now of the order of 'a buzzing fly'. Also rendered insignificant are Andrei's Napoleonic dreams of earthly glory and personal success, which he had used to justify leaving his pregnant wife and going off to war. Andrei contemplates the little icon of Jesus that his sister had given him, telling him that it would protect him 'against his will'. He wishes that he could say, 'Lord, have mercy on me...' But proud Andrei is not able to humble himself in this way. Still, Andrei's brush with death gives him insight into what really matters—and what does not (1.3:19, 309–13).

Andrei, reported missing in action, returns home to his family estate just as his wife Liza is in labour. He shows signs of a softened heart when he greets his wife, using an endearment and saying 'God is merciful...', words that he wished he could say, but was unable to say at Austerlitz. However, Liza dies in childbirth. Her dead face seems to say, 'I love you all, and have done no harm to anyone; and what have you done to me?' (2.1:9, 350–1). Tolstoy arranges this scene as if to prove the point of the proverb quoted earlier at the Rostovs' name day celebration, namely, that God can be merciful on the battlefield while death strikes at home.

Andrei's love and forgiveness in the face of death

Later in *War and Peace*, wounded in the Battle of Borodino, Andrei finds the faith that he stopped short of at Austerlitz. Andrei now is able to embrace what was embodied in the icon his sister had given him: 'yes, that love which God preached on earth, which Princess Marya taught me, and which I didn't understand.' He forgives his former rival Anatole Kuragin and weeps 'tender loving tears for his fellow men, for himself, and for his own and their errors' (3.2:37, 872–4). When by 'fate', as Andrei calls it, he is reunited with his ex-fiancée Natasha, he forgives her for breaking off their engagement (4.1:16, 1057). What the hitherto proud Andrei had seen his pious sister Marya do in life, he can only do as he is dying.

With death at hand, Andrei tries at first to think about life, death, love, and God and sort them all out in his mind. But language itself collapses, and he can only hear the rhythmic whisper of 'piti-piti' or just 'ti-ti' (3.3:32, 988–9). Despite having Natasha, Marya, and, briefly, his son at his bedside, in his final weeks Andrei no longer feels love for flesh-and-blood human beings. The love he feels is transcendent (Figure 4). He associates it with the love preached in the Gospels: 'Love is God, and to die means that I, a particle of love, shall return to the general and eternal source.' Then he experiences death as a dreadful something that is standing behind the door or else trying to break in. Then he feels a 'veil' lifting 'from his spiritual vision'. Ultimately, he experiences death as an 'awakening from sleep' and 'an awakening from life'. Natasha is left to ask, 'Where has he gone? Where is he now?...' (4.1:16, 1058–61).

Critics and readers marvelled at how Tolstoy describes what dying feels like to the person who is dying, an experience that, by

4. Natasha at the deathbed of Andrei in *War and Peace*, illustration by Leonid Pasternak.

definition, cannot be known. 'How does Count Tolstoy know this?' his contemporaries asked. The critic Mikhail Bakhtin ascribed to Tolstoy a 'passion' for depicting death. But depicting death itself is only the culmination of Tolstoy's depiction of lives lived in death's shadow.

Deaths among the Rostovs

In *War and Peace*, the Rostov family suffers death in different forms and at different ages. When the Countess Rostov is introduced in the novel, Tolstoy mentions in passing that she is 'evidently worn out with child-bearing—she had had twelve' (1.1:7, 37). At this point in 1805, only four of her children are alive: Vera, Nikolai, Natasha, and Petya. The reader is left to do the maths. Eight Rostov children must have died as babes or children. But Tolstoy says no more. The Rostovs are living proof of the precariousness of life from womb, to nursery, to battlefield, and beyond.

This gives added poignancy to his parents' anxiety when the teenage Petya, caught up in patriotic fervour and tsar-worship, wants to enlist in the army. After his parents initially refuse to grant their permission, Petya threatens that he will run away and his father gives in, attempting to get him set up 'in some less dangerous place' (3.1:21, 725). But when Petya is sent by the general of his regiment to deliver a message to a partisan detachment, he joins them in their guerrilla action and is killed.

In this segment involving the death of Petya Rostov and his mother's grief, Tolstoy conjures up situations and moods that recall the epics of Homer and Virgil when they introduce into tales of military triumph a voice of regret at the loss of human life. The death of Petya Rostov clearly reveals in Tolstoy's epic rendering of Russian victory in 1812 the germs of his later full-scale rejection of old lies about the glory of dying for one's country.

Petya's death devastates his parents. In the epilogue of *War and Peace* Tolstoy reports that Count Rostov died in 1812, with Petya's death one of 'the events of the past year...that fell, like one blow after another, on the old count's head' (Epilogue 1:5, 1225). His son's death pushes the count closer to death. Petya's mother rallies, thanks in part to Natasha, who had been grieving for Andrei but now comforts her grieving mother. However, at the very end, in 1820, Countess Rostov lives on in a condition that Tolstoy describes in brutal terms: 'She ate, drank, slept, or kept awake, but did not live.... She wanted nothing from life but tranquility, and that tranquility only death could give her.' In this prolonged state of living death she is prone to bouts of anger, but all who love her exchange knowing glances that say 'that it was a joy...to restrain oneself for the sake of this being, once so dear, once as full of life as we, and now so pathetic, *Memento mori* [remember that you too will die]—said these glances' (Epilogue 1:13,1252–3). As they show compassion for the dying countess, the remaining Rostovs show they have learned to live in the shadow of death (Box 2).

Memento mori in *Anna Karenina*

Anna Karenina is a *memento mori* in the form of a novel. From
the death of a stranger on the railroad tracks (by suicide? by
accident?) that greets Anna when she arrives in Moscow and
haunts her dreams ever after, to Dolly mourning over her dead
baby boy, to Levin hiding a rope and his hunting rifle lest he be
tempted to kill himself in the final part of the novel, Tolstoy makes
Anna Karenina into more than a novel of adultery and family life.
It is a meditation on death and mortality.

In his *Diary of a Writer*, Dostoevsky described how *Anna
Karenina* was starting to seem banal to him, but that all this
changed when he read 'the scene of the heroine's death'.
Dostoevsky had in mind not Anna's death on the train track but
the scene midway through the novel when Anna nearly dies after
giving birth to her lover Vronsky's child. Both Vronsky and her
husband Karenin are at her bedside. Dostoevsky praised Tolstoy
for revealing 'a great and eternal living truth'. 'These petty,
insignificant and deceitful beings suddenly become genuine and
truthful people, worthy of being called men, solely because of a
natural law, the law of human death. Their shell vanished, and

truth alone appeared.' As Dostoevsky tells it, even Vronsky, whom he regarded as a 'stallion in a uniform', becomes fully human in the valley of the shadow of death.

Anna, suffering from puerperal fever—which, according to the doctors, 'ends in death in ninety-nine cases out of a hundred'—begs for Karenin's forgiveness and then asks him to take Vronsky's hand and forgive him too (4:17, 417). Karenin, overwhelmed with 'a joyous feeling of love and forgiveness of his enemies', begins to sob 'like a child' (4:17, 416). According to Matthew Arnold, one of the first English critics to write about *Anna Karenina*, had this been 'a common novel', by which he presumably means the kind of novels that Victorian readers were used to, 'the story would have ended there'. But just as 'the story does not always end so in life', so too does it go on in Tolstoy's novel.

When Anna, against all odds, escapes death and life goes on, what happens to the love and forgiveness that she, Karenin, and Vronsky experienced when she was on that line between life and death where, in Tolstoy's universe, earthly systems and values cease to matter? As Anna recovers, her passion for Vronsky returns. Meanwhile, Karenin surrenders to what Tolstoy calls 'that primitive force' that rules and orders life around him (4:19, 422, 426; 4:22, 434). He feels compelled to do what society expects of a cuckold rather than acting according to what he had felt in his heart when Anna's life hung in the balance.

However, Vronsky seems not to revert back to being that 'stallion in uniform'. There are signs that he is now more fully human in that he is aware of his own mortality and fears dying without leaving a trace. Nonetheless, he focuses less on his immortal soul than on achieving immortality in more tangible forms: once back from Italy, he erects a hospital for the local peasants, which Anna slyly suggests to Dolly is 'a monument he will be leaving behind here'. And he now wants Anna to get divorced so that they can marry (6:20, 625). Vronsky knows that only then would future children bear his name and carry on the Vronsky line.

After she recovers from puerperal fever, Anna lives out her passion for Vronsky. At first, she does so happily, during their time together in Italy. However, she becomes increasingly miserable after their return to Russia, where she suffers because she is separated from her son Seryozha, who is in Karenin's custody, and because she is isolated from other loved ones. She yearns for the love and forgiveness she experienced when she lay dying, but she is unable to return those feelings. She feels a void that she desperately attempts to fill with sex, with morphine, and with other diversions, of which she says, 'it's all just a deception, it's all just morphine under another name' (7:12, 707).

As he struggled to finish *Anna Karenina* in the midst of his own spiritual crisis, Tolstoy was inspired by the 17th-century religious thinker Blaise Pascal. In his *Thoughts*, Pascal wrote that all mortals are left with intimations of a happiness that comes from embracing God; when mortals forsake God, they feel an 'infinite abyss' that they seek to fill, only to find that all earthly pursuits still leave them empty. Only faith will fill this abyss and make them happy. The same is true for Anna. Thus, in her last acts, when she throws herself on the train track, wants to move 'out of harm's way', cannot do it in time, and finally begs God for forgiveness, Tolstoy suggests that Anna's yearnings for love, happiness, and forgiveness created an abyss that only faith could fill (7:31, 771).

Levin and death

Meanwhile, in *Anna Karenina*'s other main plotline, Levin also reckons with death and mortality. In Part 3, he comes close to death vicariously when his dying brother Nikolai visits him. The two engage in a wordless dialogue which, had it been put into words, would have run like this. Levin: 'You're going to die, you're going to die, you're going to die!' Nikolai: 'I know I'm going to die, but I'm afraid, afraid, afraid.' The narrator tells us that this is what they *would* have said, had they 'spoken from the heart' (3:32, 353–4). But, like most human beings in Tolstoy's universe, they do not speak straight from the heart and thus do not say 'what they were really thinking and feeling'. Instead, they argue about politics. Tolstoy isolates the two brothers from each other in the face of death, thus showing the truth of Pascal's observation that 'one dies alone'.

From this point on, thoughts of his own death overwhelm Levin. As Part 3 closes, Levin encounters a cousin of Kitty's at the railway station and rambles about it being time for him to die (3:32, 355–6). And, when next seen in Part 4, Levin starts in with his friend Stiva Oblonsky about death, and how 'this whole world of ours is really but a spot of mildew which has formed on a tiny planet' (4:7, 379). But Stiva shuts him up, tells him that such talk is 'as old as the hills', and invites him to his dinner party, where Levin sees Kitty again. He proposes, for the second time, and Kitty accepts. Though genuine, Levin's love for Kitty only diverts him from the need to find meaning in life in the face of death.

In Part 5, a summons to Nikolai's deathbed marks the end of their honeymoon. Drawing on what he witnessed at his own brother's death from consumption, Tolstoy describes Nikolai's death in a chapter called 'Death' (5:20, 501–8). (This chapter stands out in *Anna Karenina* because it alone has a title.) Levin marvels at how Kitty, like his peasant nurse back home, knew 'what life was, and what death was' and how 'to deal with people who were dying' (5:19, 499). This knowledge stems from the women's faith.

Even after the birth of his son, Levin is tormented by thoughts of death. In *Anna Karenina*'s final part, after Anna's suicide, Tolstoy reveals that Levin, a seemingly 'happy family man in good health', has also contemplated suicide (8:9, 793). Indeed, on the last day of *Anna Karenina*, all human activity seems pointless to

Levin. As the peasants toil away, Levin asks, 'Why is all this being done?' 'Today or tomorrow, or in ten years' time' they'll be buried and 'nothing will be left' of them. Seeing the shadow of death everywhere, he can only ask the anguished question: 'What is the point?' (8:11, 797). Even his beloved estate seems to resemble Pascal's image of the human condition, absent faith in God: a cell where men condemned to death wait in despair for their sentences to be carried out.

Right after expressing this despair, Levin encounters a peasant whose words to him about 'obeying God's will' and 'living for the soul', as opposed to 'living for the belly', somehow suddenly awaken in Levin his latent faith in God. Levin had been searching for answers to his fear of death elsewhere, in the work of philosophers and even a theologian, but to no avail. Now he joyously recognizes he should live for God and love his neighbour and that these feelings had, without him knowing it, been instilled in him in childhood and guiding him all along. Levin thanks God for this faith, 'stifling the sobs rising within him' (8:11–12, 798–802). Levin has, on this summer's night as he gazes at the starry skies above him, been saved from an end like Anna's. Life under the shadow of death no longer seems meaningless to him.

Compassion for the dying Ivan Ilyich

In 'The Death of Ivan Ilyich' (1886), Tolstoy moves from his devastating exposé of the vanity of Ivan Ilyich's upper-class life to a revelation that compassion is all that matters in the face of death. The source of this compassion is Gerasim, a peasant servant who lovingly cares for Ivan Ilyich, the dying man. Gerasim does what he can to serve and comfort Ivan Ilyich: he holds his legs in the air to relieve the pain, empties the chamber pot, carries him, buttons his trousers, all because, as Gerasim explains, 'We've all got to die. So why grudge a little trouble?' (7, 193). 'It's God's will,' says Gerasim (1, 162).

Whereas the peasant Gerasim accepts death, living and loving others accordingly, the upper-class Ivan and his ilk do their best to ignore death and are tormented when they must face their own death or someone else's. As the story opens, Ivan's colleagues in the civil service, glad the accident happened to Ivan and not to them, wonder about the promotions that this death might bring about for them and others. His wife is concerned with increasing the pension she will receive. Ivan, for his part, could not accept that death applies personally to him, who had been 'little Vanya', with parents and loved ones and 'all the joys and sorrows and delights of childhood, boyhood, and youth' (6, 187). When he finally accepts that he is dying, Ivan Ilyich wallows in existential horror, feels sorry for himself, blames his fellow human beings and God for being cruel to him, and despairs, until eventually, he starts to accept death.

By contrast, Gerasim understands that we are all condemned to death and that the appropriate response is to show love for the dying man. And, as Tolstoy tells it, Ivan in his last moments is infected by Gerasim's compassion and feels compassion for those he leaves behind, including his wife (whom he had resented earlier). As he dies, he experiences light and joy and declares to himself 'Death is finished… It is no more' (12, 209).

The death of Leo Tolstoy

Tolstoy died of pneumonia on 7 November 1910 at a remote railway station called Astapovo. On 28 October in the night, he had left the estate where he had been born and where he and his wife Sophia had lived with their family. At various points over the years, Tolstoy had threatened to leave his wife. In 1897, he explained in a letter intended for his wife that 'like the Hindus who at age sixty retire to the forests, like every religious old man who desires to devote his last years of his life to God, and not to jokes, games, gossip and tennis', so he, approaching his seventieth year, craved rest and isolation. Although he didn't end up going that time, he did leave in 1910.

In addition to the models Tolstoy cited in his letter of Hindus and others retiring from worldly life, there were the homeless wanderers, the holy fools, the pilgrims that he, like his own mother before him, had befriended. They appear in Tolstoy's fiction, starting with Grisha the Holy Fool and 'great Christian' of *Childhood, Boyhood, Youth*. In *War and Peace*, the reader is told that Marya, the character modelled on Tolstoy's mother, once dreamed of joining the God's folk who wandered through Russia. She had even obtained a bundle of pilgrim's clothes so that she would be ready when the spirit moved her (2.3:26, 520–1). But she couldn't bring herself to leave her nephew and her father. Unlike Marya, the hero of Tolstoy's late story 'Father Sergius', disenchanted with worldly life and sex, does leave to join a monastery. Dismayed to find himself basking in the glory of his position as revered spiritual leader, he sets off one more time and finds peace as a wanderer and eventually as an exile living a simple life in Siberia.

Tolstoy's circumstances as a family man and as a public figure doomed his escape plot. In the letter he left for his wife, he apologized for leaving, said he believed he could not do otherwise, and explained briefly that he was abandoning the worldly life to live the rest of his days in solitude. After visiting his sister who was living in a convent, Tolstoy set off for an unknown destination thought by some to be Bulgaria and by others the Caucasus. He developed pneumonia and lay dying for several days in the stationmaster's quarters at Astapovo.

The enmity that had arisen over the years between his wife Sophia and his disciples—with the grown Tolstoy children caught in between or taking sides—persisted. Until the very end, Sophia, who travelled to Astapovo, was kept from his bedside lest her presence upset him. Whereas Tolstoy had hoped to live his last days in solitude and tranquillity, his death became a spectacle. Meanwhile, accounts of these last days were recorded by Tolstoy, until his strength gave out, and by those who knew him, and also by those who did not. The press reported. There were demonstrations.

Tolstoy was buried back at his estate, in the woods where his brother had said, as they played Ant Brothers as children, that the green stick was buried. This had been Tolstoy's wish. Tolstoy remained true to the ideal of the Ant Brothers: 'And just as I believed then that there was that green stick on which was written what would destroy all evil in people and give them great happiness, so do I believe even now that this truth exists and that it will be revealed to people and grant them what it promises' (34:387).

When he and his siblings first cleaved together as children they already had inklings of the fact that 'the angel of death' was hovering over their lives. They yearned for love and for an end to sorrow. When Tolstoy contemplated his own end—and his eventual burial—he wanted to return to the site he associated with these feelings. As Tolstoy's fictional heroes reckon with the angel of death—on the bastions of Sevastopol, on the battlefield of Borodino, in the throes of childbirth, in the sick room, in the fields and woods, or on the railroad track—Tolstoy often brings out the Ant Brother in them too: all they want is for everyone to love and to forgive.

Chapter 5
What Tolstoy believed

As he approached the age of 50, Tolstoy experienced what is often described as a spiritual crisis. He struggled to finish *Anna Karenina*. Once the novel was done, Tolstoy devoted the next several years to religious life. As a first step, he attempted to return to the fold of the Russian Orthodox Church and to share in the faith of the Russian folk. But he soon doubted the Church's doctrines, rituals, and practices. So Tolstoy struck out on his own to identify what he thought was the essence of Jesus's teachings. For him, the core (shared with other world religions) was the call to love others and God. Tolstoy produced a series of religious and theological works that included, in close succession from 1879 to 1884, his *Confession, An Examination of Dogmatic Theology, Translation and Harmonization of the Gospels, The Gospel in Brief,* and *What I Believe* (sometimes translated as *My Religion*). These were followed up a decade later by *The Kingdom of God Is Within You*, in which he expands on his doctrine of non-resistance to evil.

For several years after *Anna Karenina*, Tolstoy wrote largely on religious topics. Before his death in 1883, fellow Russian novelist Ivan Turgenev wrote to Tolstoy that his own 'song was sung', but that Tolstoy should go back to writing fiction. Although Turgenev did not live to read it, Tolstoy continued, fitfully, to write fiction that included the masterpieces 'Death of Ivan

Ilyich' (1885) and 'Hadji Murat' (written between 1896 and 1904; published 1912) (Figure 5).

Still, writing fiction mattered less than before. In *What I Believe*, Tolstoy described how his outlook on life had changed so that he 'ceased to desire what [he] had previously desired'

5. **Tolstoy at work in 1891, by Ilya Repin.**

(Introduction, 307). Being an author, along with other forms of earthly success, didn't seem important. In his later *What Is Art?* (1897), Tolstoy argued that art should be accessible to all and should promote love of God and neighbour. The handful of novels that Tolstoy approved of were by George Eliot, Fyodor Dostoevsky, Charles Dickens, Victor Hugo, and Harriet Beecher Stowe. Tolstoy consigned his own fiction 'to the category of bad art', with the exception of his 'Prisoner of the Caucasus' and 'God Sees the Truth But Waits', two stories from the early 1870s written with a broader readership already in mind.

In his religious writings, Tolstoy worked in a variety of genres (novels, stories, parables, tracts, treatises, letters). He had long been active in the education of the peasants and promotion of literacy and continued on that front by writing stories 'for the people', that is, for the Russian folk. And he was also writing increasingly for a global public: this was the literary front of his campaign to break down national boundaries and to promote universal brotherhood.

The religion of Jesus, cleansed of dogma and mysticism

Tolstoy's turn to religion in the late 1870s seemed to mark a break in his life. Tolstoy himself at times presented it that way. But what happened was the fruition of what had been developing, fitfully, over the years. From his youth on, Tolstoy had gone through periods of religious enquiry and spiritual yearning, which he recorded in his diaries and letters. The beliefs that he articulated later had been foreshadowed and even tried out over the years in his fiction.

During the siege of Sevastopol in 1855, in the fifth week of Lent, Tolstoy—then aged 26—recorded in his diary that a conversation he had had about God had given him the idea of 'a new religion': 'the religion of Jesus, cleansed of dogma and mysticism, a practical religion, not promising future bliss, but giving bliss on earth' (47:37). Tolstoy eventually devoted himself to realizing this very idea. Thus, as Tolstoy indicates by the title *The Kingdom of God Is Within You*, God's kingdom is ready to be realized now, on this earth, rather than in the future in an unknown realm. And the subtitle of this same work—*Christianity Not as a Mystical Religion But as a New Concept of Life*—harks back to that plan to 'cleans[e] the religion of Jesus of dogma and mysticism and mak[e] it practical'.

As Tolstoy put it later, one has to choose between the Creed (which sets forth Christian doctrine, including miracles, which Tolstoy rejected) and the Sermon on the Mount (which contains the heart of Jesus's teachings, including the call to turn the other cheek, to love one's enemy, and to judge not). 'One cannot believe in both' (*Kingdom of God*, 3, 75). He chose the Sermon on the Mount and built his faith on that.

Throughout his fiction, Tolstoy shows his characters attending liturgies and partaking in the sacraments of the Russian Orthodox Church with mixed feelings. In *Childhood*, Nikolai Irtenev gets no comfort from the prayers over his mother's corpse during the memorial service (27, 105); in *Youth*, in a burst of religious yearning, he attempts to take the sacrament of confession seriously, only to find himself in a vicious circle when, after confessing, he feels pride at his zeal, and then feels compelled to go back and confess all over again (7–8, 230–5). Tolstoy repeats this pattern elsewhere, when a turn to traditional forms of piety gives way to disillusionment.

Tolstoy's critique of church ritual in his fiction culminated in his lampoon of the Eucharist in his late novel *Resurrection*, about which his wife wrote in her diary: 'I was copying the revised proofs of *Resurrection* for Lev Nikolaevich, and was repelled by the calculated cynicism of his description of the Orthodox service. For instance: "The priest extended to the people the gilt image of the cross on which Jesus Christ was executed—*instead of the gallows.*" The sacrament he calls "*kvass* soup in a cup". It's scurrilous and cynical, a crude insult to those who believe in it, and I hate it.' At this point Tolstoy saw the Eucharist as a meaningless ritual and let it show.

In *Anna Karenina*, Tolstoy embeds a critique of Russian Orthodox piety in the episode describing Kitty undergoing a religious awakening as she starts to read the Gospels on her own. For the first time, she finds a religion that seems to answer the yearnings of her soul. Piety had consisted of attending 'liturgy and all-night vigil at the Widows' Home, where one could meet one's friends, and in learning Old Church Slavonic texts by heart with a priest' (2:33, 227). But, inspired by the Gospels, Kitty takes seriously the call to love her neighbour and seems to have intuitively understood what would become a refrain in Tolstoy's later religious writings: Jesus truly meant what he said.

When her mother worries that Kitty is taking her new 'spiritual awakening' too far, Kitty makes no reply and instead thinks 'in her soul that one could never be excessive where Christianity was concerned. What could possibly be excessive about following a teaching which commands that when you are struck on one cheek, you should turn the other, and give up your tunic if someone takes your cloak?' (2:33, 228). Yet, before long, Kitty reverts to the more comfortable and less demanding Russian Orthodox faith of her girlhood, and ends up as Levin's wife and mother to their son. Kitty's short-lived religious awakening exemplifies Tolstoy's intuition, which only later became a conviction, that taking Jesus's teaching seriously calls for a radical break from the usual patterns of life—and of novelistic plots.

Russian Orthodox doctrine and practice at odds with Jesus's teaching

Tolstoy's *Confession*, the first of his religious works, goes over territory familiar from his fiction. As he describes his own lapse from childhood faith, Tolstoy subjects to scathing analysis the milieu he lived in, much as he had done in his fiction from *Childhood, Boyhood, Youth* to *Anna Karenina*. Like his forerunners in the confessional genre—such as Augustine, Rousseau, and Dostoevsky's fictional underground man—Tolstoy not only confesses his own sins, but also indicts others around him for being just as bad, or worse.

As a child, boy, and youth, he lacked role models and guidance. In *Confession*, Tolstoy describes how a friend told him that God did not exist, and how his brothers took him to a prostitute. And even his aunt, regarded as the most pious of women, encouraged him to have an affair with a married woman of status because nothing so formed a young man as much as an affair. And her dreams for his future were all of earthly success: she wanted him to be an adjutant and make a good match, which to her meant a bride with a lot of serfs. Tolstoy cites this as one of countless examples of how the 'conduct' of the Russian Orthodox believers of his class was at odds with Jesus's teachings.

Tolstoy's *Confession* reveals that he parcelled out to his fictional characters aspects of his own religious experience. There is substantial overlap with Levin, often seen as a stand-in for Tolstoy in *Anna Karenina* (for Levin's spiritual crisis, see Chapter 4 'Levin and death'). Tolstoy also imparted to his characters religious feelings and insights that he himself would later develop into precepts. Toward the end of his *Confession*, he describes how, after joyfully returning to the community of the Church, he had to distance himself, not simply because of his lack of faith in the miracles and rites, but also because he became convinced that violence, including state-sanctioned violence such as war and executions that were condoned and at times promoted by the Russian Orthodox Church, violated Jesus's teachings.

In *War and Peace*, Tolstoy shows Pierre and Natasha each register—and be disturbed by—acts done in the name of Christ that violate their intuitive sense of those teachings. Pierre is disturbed that 'We all profess the Christian law of forgiveness of injuries and love of our neighbors, the law in the honor of which we have built in Moscow forty times forty churches—but yesterday a deserter was knouted to death and a minister of that same law of love and forgiveness, a priest, gave the soldier a cross to kiss before his execution' (2.5:1, 576–78). And Natasha is disturbed when in church a prayer is suddenly read 'for the deliverance of Russia from hostile invasion' (by Napoleon). This prayer calls for 'trampling enemies under foot'. Natasha experiences a cognitive dissonance since, before this interruption of the liturgy, she had just joined the congregation in prayer 'for those who hate us' and had been experiencing the joy of forgiving her enemies (3.1:18, 709–12). Tolstoy thus attributes to Natasha, if only in this brief moment, a revelation of what became for him a major stumbling block. In fact, a diary entry of 22 May 1878, written when Russia was at war in the Balkans, shows his life imitating his art: he wrote of going to church, finding meaning in the liturgy, except for the part about 'trampling enemies', which he found to be 'blasphemy. A Christian should pray for his enemies, not against them.' In his later years, Tolstoy openly criticized the Church for supporting executions, wars, and other forms of violence.

As Tolstoy often put it, the Church, in cahoots with the government, 'hypnotized' the people into believing its false interpretations of God's message. Tolstoy offered a glimpse of how this played out in a letter he wrote (in English) to Gandhi on 7 September 1910. He reported a story about girls being examined by an archbishop on the Russian Orthodox catechism in a school in Moscow. They were being quizzed on the Ten Commandments. After the sixth was recited, the archbishop asked, 'Is it always and in every case forbidden by the law of God to kill?' Tolstoy explained to Gandhi that the girls had been 'misled by their instructor' and were supposed to answer, according to the catechism, 'Not always, for it is permissible in war and at executions.' But one young girl,

Tolstoy reports, blushed and 'answered decidedly and with emotion—"Always!" And despite all the customary sophistries of the archbishop she held steadfastly to it—that to kill is under all circumstances forbidden in the Old Testament, and that Christ has not only forbidden us to kill, but in general to do any harm to our neighbor.'

This girl is the last in Tolstoy's line of children who see and say the truth, putting to shame the lying grown-ups around them. And Tolstoy found in her statement proof of his argument that Jesus's teaching had been obscured and distorted by dogma and doctrine. Jesus's line about God the Father 'revealing unto babes' what he 'had hid from the wise and prudent' (Matthew 11:25) had a natural appeal for Tolstoy. It had been at the heart of his ethics and poetics throughout his works.

Tolstoy's gospel

Tolstoy went back to the Gospel texts, studying them in the Greek, reading commentaries, and checking different editions. Taking into account that the four canonical Gospels were chosen from a host of different accounts of what Jesus said and did, Tolstoy set about to extract what *he* determined to be the true teachings of Jesus. Tolstoy's work on the Gospels resulted in a longer *Translation and Harmonization of the Gospels* and a shorter spin-off called *The Gospel in Brief*.

Just as in *Anna Karenina*, where the artist Mikhailov declares, as he paints Christ before Pontius Pilate, that he 'could not paint a Christ who was not in [his] soul', so too did Tolstoy need to write a Christ who spoke to him—and for him (5:12, 477). This Jesus reveals the state of Tolstoy's heart. Tolstoy not only gets rid of mystery and miracle, he also makes Jesus no more the 'son of God' than the rest of us. For Tolstoy, what was special about Jesus was his genius as teacher and interpreter of God's truth.

Tolstoy was not interested in the historical Jesus. Nor was he interested in the idea that Jesus had a miraculous birth or rose to heaven. Nor was he even seeking a friend in Jesus, to help him bear his sins and griefs. As Tolstoy put it, according to one memoirist, 'what is the point of knowing that Christ went out to relieve himself? What do I care that he was resurrected? So he was resurrected—so what? God be with him! For me the important question is what am I to do, how am I to live.'

Tolstoy extracted from Jesus's teaching a set of five simple 'rules' that told Tolstoy how to live. Tolstoy's rules are: (1) don't be angry, forgive offences, live in peace; (2) do not commit adultery or debauchery, no divorce; (3) do not take oaths (such as of allegiance to a government); (4) judge not, do not punish, do not return evil for evil, avoid all violence; (5) love your neighbours, have no enemies, make no distinctions between nations. This act of reducing Jesus's teachings to a set of rules felt like a violation of the spirit of Jesus's teaching to many believers. But Tolstoy liked it. If only everyone would follow these rules, 'all men will be brothers, and everyone will be at peace with others', he wrote, and 'the kingdom of God will have come' (*What I Believe*, 6, 406). This is the green stick which the Ant Brothers had dreamed of.

As he retells and comments on the Gospels, Tolstoy discards what he regards as obscure or spurious, which tended to be anything that he thought the Church had added to support its doctrine or its programme—or, worse, the agenda of those in power. Tolstoy places the emphasis on what he considers to be important, namely, Jesus's own words. As Ernest Howard Crosby, an American inspired by Tolstoy's religious teachings, put it, 'when he does not like a verse he simply leaves it out, a wonderfully simple expedient'. Still, Crosby continues, 'the fact remains that his dramatic quality of mind has enabled him to enter into the spirit of the Gospel narrative as few other writers have done. He describes the events as if they had occurred in Moscow to-day, and we see with new insight why the Pharisees spake thus and why the disciples made such and such an answer.'

To create this effect, Tolstoy introduced some features of his Russian readers' reality into the text of the Gospels. Thus, for example, he substituted Russian 'kopecks' for 'coins'. He refers to the 'steppes of Judaea'. And, in a particularly pointed word choice, Tolstoy translates 'the Pharisees' as ' the orthodox', in order to put the Russian Orthodox on the spot for their hypocrisy. For example, where Luke's Jesus says: 'you Pharisees make clean the outside of the cup and the platter; but your inward part is full of ravening and wickedness' (Luke 11:39), Tolstoy's Jesus says: 'You Orthodox people wash everything outside, but is everything clean with you?' (2, 50). What Tolstoy does with the Gospels is a variant of the defamiliarization or estrangement that Viktor Shklovsky identified in Tolstoy's fiction (see Chapter 7, 'Defamiliarization or "looking at things afresh"'). The aim was to get readers to take a new, fresh look at a phenomenon. This meant getting rid of old interpretative habits and de-automatizing perception. Tolstoy does just that with the Gospels.

In a pamphlet called 'How to Read the Gospels', Tolstoy offered explicit instructions on how to approach the canonical Gospels and find one's own truth there. He advised readers to 'put aside foregone conclusions' and not to be concerned if much is incomprehensible. Readers should take a blue pen and underline all that is clear and comprehensible to them, then take a red pen and underline all that Jesus actually said. Then readers should focus (only) on what ends up doubly underscored—in both red and blue. While Tolstoy allowed for differences in what different people would find unintelligible, he was confident that if readers followed this programme, they would arrive at the essence of Jesus's teachings. For Tolstoy, this do-it-yourself approach with blue and red ink was better than what was officially taught. As he wrote in the introduction to *What I Believe*, 'not all can be initiated into the deepest mysteries of dogmatics, homiletics, patristics, liturgics, hermeneutics, apologetics, etc., but all may and should understand what Christ said to all the millions of simple, unlearned people who have lived and are living' (Introduction, 308).

'But who is my neighbour?'

Love of neighbour is a tenet of many ethical systems, but there has been a variety of interpretations of what this love entails and who one's neighbour is. Tolstoy warns: 'Ratiocination about who my neighbor is is a trap that lures away from the truth and, in order not to fall into it, one must not reason, but act.' Tolstoy's ultimate advice is that one should love in the here and now. This means forgetting about one's self and one's own interests and not making distinctions between one's own and other people.

Tolstoy had explored this vexed question in his fiction. Platon Karataev in *War and Peace* stands out as someone who just knows who his neighbour is—and loves accordingly. His love knows no distinction based on class, creed, nation, or species: Platon 'loved his dog, his comrades, the French, and Pierre'. Platon's love is active. He feeds, clothes, comforts, and inspires those around him. And yet he 'had no attachments, friendships, or love, as Pierre understood them'. And 'in spite of Karataev's affectionate tenderness for him...he would not have grieved for a moment at parting from [Pierre]' (4.1:13, 1047). Platon is seen practising this neighbourly love only under special circumstances, as a prisoner of war.

Tolstoy punctuates the rest of *War and Peace* with conflicts that arise as his heroes are torn between love of neighbour and love of their own kin. For example, as the Rostovs flee burning Moscow, Natasha impulsively orders carts filled with their worldly possessions to be emptied and used to transport wounded soldiers, to her mother's chagrin. (Still, Tolstoy does not allow this triumph of neighbourly love to be its own reward. Natasha's cousin Sonya manages to salvage some of their goods, and

Natasha finds herself rewarded when, by chance or fate, Andrei Bolkonsky is among the wounded.) Years later, as the epilogue ends, Pierre is involved in political action for his neighbour and Marya torments herself with not loving all as Christ commanded (see Chapter 3, 'Courtship, marriage, and family happiness in *War and Peace*').

The conflict between love of neighbour and love of one's own that Tolstoy explored in his fiction came home to roost at his estate Yasnaya Polyana. In notes made in 1881, Tolstoy's wife Sophia recorded that, in the period after *Anna Karenina*, when Tolstoy was immersed in religion, he said that he had seen 'the light' and that this changed his relationship to others: whereas 'before there had been a defined circle of *his* people, those near and dear' as neighbours, now 'millions of people had become his brothers'. Tolstoy had taken to heart the dream of the Ant Brothers. And Tolstoy expected his nearest and dearest—his wife, first and foremost—to adjust.

In his *Gospel in Brief*, which he finished in 1883, Tolstoy signals his new view of this wide-reaching type of neighbourly love. Before retelling the parable of the Good Samaritan (Luke 10:25–35), Tolstoy offers a preamble warning against the 'temptation...to consider it one's duty to do good only to one's fellow-countrymen and to regard other nations as enemies'. Then, where Luke has 'you shall love...your neighbour as yourself', Tolstoy's Jesus extrapolates 'love...your brothers, [God's] sons, whether they are your countrymen or not'. (Tolstoy thus avoids even using the word neighbour since it is open to so many different interpretations.) After telling the parable of the Samaritan who helps the Jew left half-dead on the side of the road, Tolstoy ends by stating the moral: 'see that you too behave like that to foreigners' (9, 230).

As Tolstoy makes clear in *What I Believe*, Jesus's commandment to love one's enemies and to make no distinction between one's fellow-countrymen and others means that one should not distinguish between one's own nation and other nations. In the end, Tolstoy believed that such distinctions are pernicious: the 'gross fraud called patriotism and love of one's country' leads to enmity between nations and to war. Whereas before he had been deluded into thinking that his 'welfare [was] bound up only with that of the people of [his] own nation', he now understood that his welfare was bound up with 'that of all the peoples of the earth' (12, 532–3).

What Jesus meant by 'judge not'

In *What I Believe*, Tolstoy describes his efforts to determine what Jesus really meant by 'judge not, and ye shall not be judged; condemn not, and ye shall not be condemned' (Luke 6:37). These words were usually taken to mean that 'one must not speak ill of one's neighbour' or judge one's neighbour in one's heart. Tolstoy, however, began to suspect that what Jesus really meant was that 'one must not set up law courts, nor judge one's neighbour in them'. After examining different editions of the Greek texts, Tolstoy concluded that Jesus was in fact forbidding participation in these judicial and penal systems, which, as Tolstoy observes, inflict untold suffering and are an evil both for those condemned to punishment *and* for those who judge and condemn them. From then on, he spoke out against the system and refused to serve when summoned for jury duty in 1883.

Back in *Childhood*, Grisha the Holy Fool had spoken out—in his mysterious way—against human beings punishing other human beings. The serfs of Nikolai's father let loose their dogs on Grisha so that they will maul him and keep him away from the house. In his uncanny mode of speech, Grisha raves about this, noting that the dogs wanted to bite him to death and that it was 'a great sin' to set the dogs on him. But Grisha also begs the master *not* to punish the serfs for this (5, 23). He rejects all forms of earthly punishments, including in this case a master punishing his own serfs, which according to the earthly system he had the right to do.

Grisha thus anticipates Tolstoy's later understanding of what 'turning the other cheek' and 'judge not' really mean.

Tolstoy's final novel, *Resurrection*, is a denunciation of the Russian courts and prisons. As he reveals the cruelty, injustice, and suffering inflicted on the prisoners, Tolstoy novelizes his understanding of 'judge not'. As Nekhlyudov, the hero, moves from being a member of a jury responsible for a wrongful conviction to becoming a self-appointed prisoners' advocate, he asks 'a very simple question: Why, and by what right, do some people lock up, torment, exile, flog, and kill others, while they are themselves just like those whom they torment, flog, and kill?' (2:30, 340). Later, Nekhlyudov notes that the 'eternal, immutable law written by God in the hearts of human beings' tells them that they should treat each other with love and fellow-feeling. But once you accept that there are 'circumstances when one may deal with other human beings without love', there is 'no limit' to the horrors that can be committed and to the suffering they bring to all (2:40, 382–3).

Non-violence in Gethsemane, at Yasnaya Polyana, and beyond

Reinforcing his insistence on universal love and non-judgement was Tolstoy's conviction that 'Jesus really meant what he said' when he prohibited violence in any shape or form. Tolstoy works from the Sermon on the Mount (Matthew 5:38–48), where Jesus replaces 'an eye for eye' with the commandment to 'resist not evil', to 'turn the other cheek', and says to 'love your enemies, bless them that curse you, do good to them that hate you, and pray for them which despitefully use you, and persecute you', thus becoming 'children of the Father who is in heaven'.

In his *Gospel in Brief*, Tolstoy shows that Jesus was tempted to resort to violence rather than surrender to death without a fight. In Luke 22:36, Tolstoy's Jesus tells his 'pupils' (Tolstoy's term for disciples) to 'get knives that we may not perish uselessly' (10, 244).

Commenting on this passage in *Translation and Harmonization of the Gospels*, Tolstoy claims Jesus was clearly intending to use violence to defend himself. Tolstoy chides the church interpreters for trying to explain away this fact (by making the call to arms figurative, for example). For Tolstoy Jesus's despair and temptation were critical.

Only when Jesus retreats alone into the Garden of Gethsemane to pray to his Father does he overcome the temptation to fight. He then embraces his Father's way, which is non-violent. And, as Tolstoy explains, what Jesus lived through, from initial temptation to resist evil with violence to his eventual decision not to use violence, makes the love he preaches in his 'farewell discourse' (or at the Last Supper) a more powerful example for others to follow.

What would it mean to live out Jesus's teaching in the real world? As Tolstoy explains in *What I Believe*, the message is clear and simple: 'never do violence, never do an act that is contrary to love, and if they insult you, bear the insult and still do not inflict violence on anyone else' (2, 321). He notes that although he had been brought up to accept Christ's teaching as divine, nobody seemed to take it seriously: he was taught to retaliate, to seek revenge, to go to war.

Violence or its threat is what ruled and ran the world he lived in: 'all my circumstances, my tranquility, the safety of myself and my family and my property were all based on the law repudiated by Christ, on the law of a tooth for a tooth' (2, 323). In the rousing last chapter of *The Kingdom of God Is Within You*, Tolstoy writes: 'We cannot pretend that we do not see the armed policeman who marches up and down beneath our windows to guarantee our security while we eat our luxurious dinner, or look at the new piece at the theater, or that we are unaware of the existence of the soldiers who will make their appearance with guns and cartridges directly our property is attacked.' Nor can we deny that 'there are a hundred thousand men in prison in Russia alone to guarantee the security of our property and tranquility...' (12, 346).

Did Tolstoy really mean no violence ever? Was this possible? As memoirs left by those who visited Tolstoy attest, his interlocutors, convinced that even Tolstoy would agree to the use of force in certain circumstances, would test him with horrific scenarios, involving the slaughter and violation of innocents, asking what he would do. Tolstoy was always ready with his counter-arguments and refused to back down from his ideal. As he saw it, Jesus was serious about never, ever, using violence. That was the ideal and Tolstoy would not compromise on it.

Meanwhile, Tolstoy made attempts to practise his ideal of non-resistance to evil by force on the local level, at his estate Yasnaya Polyana. Ernest Howard Crosby relates a story that he heard from the Swiss governess when he visited Yasnaya Polyana in 1894: Tolstoy's youngest daughter had been playing with a peasant boy who hit her very hard with a stick. She ran to find her father, wanting him to punish the boy. Tolstoy explained to her that were he to whip the boy, the boy would hate the two of them and that it was better to make him love them. So he suggested that little Alexandra get the jam pot from the pantry and offer the boy some jam. Crosby imagined that the jam 'would have kindled into a flame' 'the spark of love' that was in that boy and that is in all boys. Still, he admitted that he didn't know how this 'experiment in penology' turned out.

Crosby reports that once when he told this story to an audience in New Jersey, a gentleman spoke up from the back to say that he knew what the boy would do next. 'He would come up to the house the next day and hit her on the other arm.' Crosby writes that between these two gentlemen, the one from Russia and the other from New Jersey, 'lies all the debatable land of human conduct. Which of the two was more deeply versed in the nature of man, and is the jam or the stick, forgiveness or punishment, vengeance or love, the better civilizer? There is certainly an element of beauty in this little incident, and can there be beauty without truth? And if there is truth in the Russian point of view, is it not a truth that can be applied far more frequently in our daily lives and in our institutions which express them?'

The impact of Tolstoy's religious works

Suppressed in Russia, Tolstoy's religious works were printed abroad and made their way back illicitly. These works, along with others that followed, especially his late novel *Resurrection*, showed him to be an outspoken critic of the Russian Orthodox Church and also of the Russian state—indeed of all states, since all practised violence. In 1901, the Russian Orthodox Church excommunicated Tolstoy, an act that spurred demonstrations throughout Russia. As the world watched (and many protested), a man recognized as one of the period's greatest moral thinkers was declared an apostate. Alexey Suvorin, an influential editor of *New Times*, spoke for many Russians, from all walks of life, when he declared: 'We have two tsars: Nicholas II and Leo Tolstoy.'

Tolstoy's religious works were translated and read around the world. Constance Garnett translated Tolstoy's *The Kingdom of God Is Within You* in 1894 (before she set about translating the fiction of Turgenev, Dostoevsky, and Tolstoy). Mohandas Gandhi reported having been 'overwhelmed' by *The Kingdom of God Is Within You*, which he read in 1894 while in South Africa. He admired Tolstoy for his 'independent thinking, profound morality, and truthfulness'. Tolstoy influenced Gandhi as he developed his own programme of non-violent action.

When Vladimir Chertkov, a close disciple of Tolstoy, was exiled from Russia in 1897, he was active in publishing and propagating Tolstoy's teachings in England. Writing in 1902, John Coleman Kenworthy, an Englishman who fervently supported Tolstoy's views, compared Tolstoy's impact to that of religious figures like

John Wesley, founder of Methodism, and John Bunyan, author of *Pilgrim's Progress*.

Tolstoy's late works made 'Tolstoyans' out of many, in Russia and abroad. They took his version of the Christian religion ('cleansed of dogma and mysticism') to heart and tried to live accordingly. Some of them banded together in communes, their goal to put 'Tolstoyism' into practice. Tolstoy himself was wary of any attempt to make an '-ism' out of his teaching or to organize intentional communities. What mattered to Tolstoy was what went on in the individual conscience. This is in keeping with his belief that 'the kingdom of God is within you' (Luke 17:21), which for him meant that each person needs to recognize and profess the truth found within. To this end, Tolstoy hoped that his religious works would get people to 'bethink themselves' (Box 3).

Box 3 'Bethink yourselves!'

Tolstoy works this phrase into a number of his late works and also used it as the title of his 1904 anti-war treatise (mentioned at the end of Chapter 2). 'Bethink yourselves' is what, in Tolstoy's rendering of the Gospels, Jesus tells his listeners at key moments, namely, in Luke 13:5, when he warns: 'Bethink yourselves or you will perish,' and in Matthew 1:15, when he commands, 'Bethink yourselves and believe in the gospel.' The verb Jesus uses in the Gospels has been traditionally translated as 'Repent' (in both Russian and English Bible translations). But 'Repent!' is a loaded command. Tolstoy avoids it. Instead he went back to the Greek verb *metanoien*, which means, simply, to change one's mind. (The Greek word consists of a root that means mind and a prefix that suggests a change of state or of place. Tolstoy makes the medium part of the message as he provides this fresh— thought-provoking—translation of a familiar word.) Tolstoy's message to his readers is: think yourselves out of that rut, open your minds to change, consider new thoughts.

This is what happened to the philosopher Ludwig Wittgenstein, who came across Tolstoy's *Gospel in Brief* by chance in a bookstore as he served in the Austrian army in 1914. He carried it with him through the war, is reported to have known whole passages by heart, and later wrote that it 'virtually kept him alive'. After the war, Wittgenstein took steps that have a Tolstoyan aura: he taught village schoolchildren and divested himself of his family fortune. And throughout the rest of his life, Tolstoy's works, not just the *Gospel* but also the fiction, remained important to him. Wittgenstein is, however, just one case. Tolstoy's religious works, whether read on their own or in conjunction with his fiction, get people thinking, not just along Tolstoy's lines but by their own lights, which was what Tolstoy was after.

Chapter 6
What then must we do?

In his later years, Tolstoy occupied himself with questions of social justice. Tolstoy wrote on a number of topics, including poverty, the allocation of goods and privileges, class relations, landownership, manual labour, famine, charity, civil disobedience, non-violence, and the ethics of diet. Tolstoy had been concerned with these questions earlier, both in his fiction and in his own life. But, inspired by his newly articulated gospel (see Chapter 5), he felt the need to address these social issues more directly. For Tolstoy, faith and action went hand in hand.

Once he had worked through the spiritual dilemmas of *What I Believe*, the natural sequel was *What Then Must We Do?* (1886). This title echoes the question posed in Luke 3:10 to John the Baptist. According to the Gospel, John replied that he who has two coats should give to him who has none, and he who has food should do the same. In *What Then Must We Do?* and subsequent works, Tolstoy came to the fore as a critic of social injustice. The other question that haunts Tolstoy's writings on inequality is, as he titled a 1902 essay, 'Need it be so?' Tolstoy uses the question to stir people up. He starts by indicating that many go along with the way of the world without even thinking about it, or else assume that nothing can be done about it anyway.

Tolstoy begins his 1902 essay by depicting two contrasting worlds that intersect briefly on a country road: that of the carriage-, horseback-, and bicycle-riding leisured class on an outing and that of the peasants, foundry workers, and factory workers. Tolstoy observes that as the members of the privileged class pass the others by, their driver threatening anyone in the way with his whip, they are 'not in the least surprised or touched' by the destitution they witness. 'They think that all this must be so' (198). As 'Need It Be So?' continues, Tolstoy encourages readers to reflect on how the privilege of some is linked to the destitution of others.

In his works on social inequality, Tolstoy does what Chekhov thought artists should do: ask questions. Tolstoy wasn't afraid to ask the tough questions. And even once he writes his way through to some answer, he continues to question. Throughout, Tolstoy uses his artistic powers—as he had done in his novels—to reveal the misery and injustice of the world around him and he uses his analytic skill to lay bare the sophistry and cruelty of the measures society takes to ignore or remedy problems.

Seeds of social conscience in Tolstoy's early fiction and life

Tolstoy's social conscience is evident in his 'autopsychological' fiction from the start. In his early *Childhood, Boyhood, Youth* (1852–6), Tolstoy chronicles his child alter ego Nikolai's dawning awareness of inequality. As he travels through the Russian countryside after his mother's funeral, Nikolai registers, as if for the first time, the existence of those living in poverty and misery. He is terrified when beggars in rags approach their carriage, asking for alms 'in the name of Christ'. They are kept at bay by a serf who has a stash of coins to dispense among them.

At another point, after joining his peers as they bully a poor foreigner who is unable to match their physical strength, Nikolai experiences a moment of remorse. In *Youth*, Nikolai tells himself he will go to church every week and spend a whole hour reading the Gospels after, then fantasizes about giving a portion of his allowance to the poor, and next wonders why servants wait on him when they, too, are human beings. But, as the chapter title— 'Daydreams'—suggests, he doesn't follow through. Tolstoy's young hero takes no real steps to alter the status quo, to protest injustice, or to change his own ways. Still, Tolstoy at least shows Nikolai registering and pondering the inequality around him. Tolstoy also makes it clear to the reader that the world he is entering grooms Nikolai to throw coins at beggars to get rid of them, to bully people who are outsiders, and to protect his privilege.

As a young landlord and serf owner, Tolstoy had moral qualms about serfdom. In March 1856, Tsar Alexander II announced that serfdom would be abolished throughout Russia in 1861. A month later, Tolstoy drafted a document that he intended to read to his serfs. In it, Tolstoy wrote: 'The Lord instilled in my soul the idea of freeing you all…' However, Tolstoy's plan came to naught. When he gathered his serfs together to propose his plan, they declined, assuming that he was swindling them and that the government plan would be more advantageous to them. During this period, Tolstoy devoted energy to educating peasants (Box 4).

Box 4 Tolstoy the teacher

After dropping out of university in 1847, Tolstoy set about educating himself and thought seriously about the process of learning. In the period right before and after the 1861 emancipation of the Russian serfs, Tolstoy was actively involved in the education of peasants, returning to an interest he had pursued briefly before. Tolstoy set up a school for peasant children, studied pedagogy, visited schools and consulted with educators in Western Europe, and published a journal dedicated

(continued)

Box 4 Continued

to pedagogy in peasant schools. As essays such as 'The School at Yasnaya Polyana' and 'Who Should Teach Whom to Write, We, the Peasant Children, or They, Us?' demonstrate, his teaching philosophy and practice were astonishingly progressive.

As he wrote his *Confession*, Tolstoy disparaged his past efforts, observing that he had been teaching 'without knowing what to teach' (3, 13). But, throughout the years, Tolstoy continued to take an active interest in the local peasant children and, as an old man, he recalled the great joy he had felt among the children.

In between *War and Peace* and *Anna Karenina*, Tolstoy had composed and compiled educational works. His efforts intensified in later years when he, together with friends and followers, published a large body of works in cheap editions for a wide readership of all ages. Tolstoy wrote works and introductions to others' work. And he also put together compendiums of stories and sayings, drawing from a variety of sources. For example, in his 1903 *Sayings by Wise Thinkers for Everyday*, two representative pages provide, in succession, excerpts from Thackeray, Lao Tse, the Talmud, Buddha, John Ruskin, the Gospel of Matthew, Muhammad, Confucius (40:202–3). These works were to educate and to open minds.

Master and peasants in the novels

From *War and Peace* through *Anna Karenina* to *Resurrection*, Tolstoy shows landowners addressing questions of distributive justice and landownership as they try to balance their own family interest and the interest of the peasants who worked the land. Serfs liberated by imperial decree in 1861 were granted small plots of land to cultivate, but they had to pay for these plots in instalments. They struggled to survive and to earn money. Many moved to cities to find work. Meanwhile, the bulk of the land still belonged to the estate owners, who then hired the peasants as labourers and/or rented out land to them.

Serfdom is a practical and moral concern in *War and Peace*, whose story begins more than fifty years before the serfs were freed. Serfs hear rumours that Napoleon, if victorious in Russia, would liberate them. The novel's masters have good intentions. Pierre Bezukhov dreams of freeing his serfs and, meanwhile, tries but fails to enact reforms for the welfare of his serfs. Inept and out of touch, Pierre is swindled by his manager and those who actually run things. His friend Andrei Bolkonsky lacks Pierre's do-gooder impulses, yet achieves results that benefit both him and the serfs.

In the epilogue, set in 1821, Pierre involves himself in political action that Tolstoy modelled on that of the Decembrists who revolted in 1825. Among the political goals of the Decembrists was the abolition of serfdom; some even envisioned radical changes to landownership that would have handed it over to the peasants. By contrast, Nikolai Rostov has compensated for his family's past profligacy by becoming an expert manager of his estate—and of his serfs. He has come to understand and to love them and their way of life. Rather than attempting to perform virtuous acts, Nikolai concerns himself with efforts that benefit his own welfare while trickling down to his serfs. Under the beneficent influence of his wife, Nikolai vows to refrain from the habit of beating his serfs when he loses his temper. (Tolstoy's diaries reveal that as a boy he had been disturbed to learn of serfs being beaten and that as a young man, in fits of anger, he, too, had beaten them.)

In *Anna Karenina*, Tolstoy shows different landowners adapting in different ways to the changes brought about by the liberation of the serfs. Vronsky, a hitherto absentee landowner, gets involved in the new local government and attempts reforms and innovations on his estate. However, he has no rapport with the peasants and no feel for farm life. He builds a state-of-the-art hospital for the peasants, but omits a maternity ward; he builds swank stables, but is stingy with the oats. By contrast, Levin is deeply attached to his family estate and has long-standing relations with the peasants. While as a bachelor he muses about starting a 'bloodless revolution' by surrendering more of his land to the peasants, he ultimately reverts, following marriage, to conventional arrangements with the peasants (3:30, 348). He consoles himself with the thought that at least he is not increasing the disparity of wealth between himself and the peasants. Much as he wants to do right by the peasants, Levin feels pressure to preserve patrimony for future generations and is not ready to divest himself of his property and wealth.

Who should own land?

Tolstoy wrestled with his own strong attachment to the land he inherited and his compulsion to buy more, on the one hand, and, on the other, anxiety about owning land, especially given his sense that the Russian peasants believed that the land should belong to all. In his diary of 1865, recording what he had 'seen in a dream', Tolstoy starts by quoting Pierre-Joseph Proudhon's phrase 'Property is theft' and ends by prophesying that, given the Russian folk's aversion to private ownership of land, 'a Russian revolution' would not be fought to overthrow 'the tsar and despotism', but rather to change the status quo in regard to landownership (48:85).

In his late novel *Resurrection*, Tolstoy addresses questions of landownership in a segment that shows the hero Nekhlyudov wondering what to do with property he has inherited. Ten years earlier, Nekhlyudov had given over to the peasants the land he inherited from his father. He has been living since then off income from his mother's considerably larger property. When she dies, Nekhlyudov faces a dilemma. He has no other income and, though childless, he feels pressure to leave the land to his sister's children. But he is convinced of 'the injustice of private land ownership'.

As Nekhlyudov weighs his options, he recalls and recites to himself the essence of the American reformer Henry George's 'brilliant' argument: 'The earth cannot be any one's property; it cannot be bought or sold any more than water, air, or sunshine. All have an equal right to the advantages it gives to men' (2:6, 239). Tolstoy was very taken with George's *Poverty and Progress* in which he argues that those who use land should pay a tax to the government for that privilege. What then must Nekhlyudov do? Though he thinks he knows what the right thing is, he hesitates to make a radical break with his way of life.

'How Much Land Does a Person Need?' (1886), one of Tolstoy's stories written for a wide readership, is a parable on private ownership of land and laying up treasures on earth. (James Joyce declared this to be 'the greatest story that the literature of the world knows'.) It tells of its hero's desperate quest to achieve happiness and security by acquiring land. The Tolstoyan moral and answer to the question posed in the title turns out to be that all the land one needs is enough for burial.

'How Much Land', like so much of Tolstoy's fiction, is 'autopsychological'. It is revealing that the terror Tolstoy experienced in 1869 at Arzamas—when the spectre of death overwhelmed and made him question his life—occurred when he was on the road scouting out land in the Penza Province. He hoped to buy it cheap and then make back his expenditure by selling timber. When Tolstoy fictionalized his Arzamas terror later in 'Notes of a Madman', the hero has a revelation that cures him of his schemes for acquiring more land. A conversation with a local peasant makes him realize that his gain would be at the price of the pain and wretchedness of the peasants.

Eventually, Tolstoy divested *himself* of his land, turning ownership over to family members. But much as Tolstoy may have hoped thus to 'unburdened, crawl toward death', like King Lear before him—in a tragedy that Tolstoy criticized but that, as George Orwell saw it, was relevant to Tolstoy's own life—his problems didn't end there. Tolstoy would live through his own version of the reckoning that Lear goes through when he takes to heart the plight of the poor and wretched around him (Act III, Scene 4).

Tolstoy and the Moscow poor

What Then Must We Do? (1886) is Tolstoy's most sustained and 'soul-stirring' response to issues of social justice. Tolstoy's project recalls Henry Mayhew's *London Labour and the London Poor* (1851) and other works in the English tradition of investigating and elucidating social problems. But Tolstoy has his own approach to observing—and reacting to—urban poverty in Moscow. He had been familiar with the hardships peasants faced in village and countryside, but had hitherto taken little notice of the plight of the poor in cities. This changed when the Tolstoy family started spending more time in Moscow in the 1880s. In *What Then Must We Do?*, Tolstoy stirs souls by indicating to his readers the direct connection between the leisure, the plenty, and the security of the 'pleasant' life that he and others enjoyed and the suffering, the want, and the precarity of the poor.

Using one of his favourite techniques (see Chapter 7, 'Hidden symmetries'), Tolstoy juxtaposes two parallel but opposite vignettes of city life at dawn in his neighbourhood in Moscow. In one, downtrodden and often depraved workers arrive at or depart from factories where they labour under exploitative and unhealthy conditions. In the other, young ladies (to Tolstoy's shame, his daughters) go off in their finery to partake in the social rituals of high society. It is revealed that the factories in the neighbourhood 'produce exclusively articles needed for balls' (stockings, silk stuffs, perfumes, and pomades). Tolstoy then notes that 'it never enters [the] heads [of the ball-goers] that there is any connection between the ball' and the drunken factory workers they see out and about. Nor do they give any thought to their coachman, an older peasant who waits in a terrible frost. (This detail recalls a motif in Russian literature and culture of the elite enjoying their lives, at the expense of peasants, as well as a story, possibly apocryphal, that circulated about his own coachman nearly freezing to death while the young Tolstoy was at a ball.) Tolstoy's purpose is to make his reader, at least, consider that there is a direct link between the suffering of the workers and the luxury and frivolity of the ball-goers (24, 187–91).

As part of his mission to educate himself about the poor of Moscow, Tolstoy involved himself in census-taking work, asking to be assigned to a slum he knew to be 'a den of most terrible poverty and vice' (4, 23). Tolstoy likens the guilt and horror he felt after seeing the slum to what he had felt when he had seen 'a man's head cut off with a guillotine' in Paris thirty years before (and had described in his *Confession*). He concludes that he was more of an aider, an abetter, and participator in the murderous poverty of Moscow than he had been as witness of the execution in Paris. He even writes that, so long as 'I have two coats and someone else has none, I share in a constantly repeated crime' (2, 13–14). This prompts him to want to take action.

When Tolstoy first set out to observe and document urban poverty, he envisioned following through with charity work to ameliorate the condition of the poor. But, as he describes in *What Then Must We Do?*, he became disillusioned with forms of charity that consist of the rich giving their surplus to the poor. Once, Tolstoy tried to tell Vasily Siutaev, a radical religious leader who had broken from the Church and disapproved of private property, that giving alms to beggars should be a good thing since 'according to the gospel, one should "clothe the naked, feed the hungry"'. But Siutaev countered that charity would not undo the existing order and was only a way for the rich to have the poor leave them alone.

Instead, Siutaev proposed to Tolstoy his more radical approach, based on active love. He suggested living and working side by side with the destitute, thus teaching and guiding them more directly (14, 82). Siutaev's arguments made Tolstoy all the more sceptical about traditional forms of benevolent charity. Tolstoy even 'came to feel that in money itself, in the very possession of it' (especially in his case, when he had not laboured to earn it), 'there is something evil and immoral' (16, 102).

Tolstoy on labour and the simple life

As Tolstoy continues *What Then Must We Do?*, he reverts, with increasing desperation, to the question 'What then must we do? What must we do?' He explains that many like him know that their 'way of life is wrong or bad', but sometimes feel 'all the same it is impossible to change it'. He describes his own 'sufferings' and 'search' for an answer (38, 304). Tolstoy writes of how reading an article by a peasant named Timofey Bondarev 'lit up the wisdom' of the biblical saying that human beings should labour by the sweat of their brow for their bread. For Tolstoy, it was important to find wisdom from those who actually tilled the soil (38, 320).

Bondarev's work, which Tolstoy helped get published, called for all to do their own labour and thus provide for themselves. Bondarev also admonished the higher classes for their 'parasitism' and for their crimes. Bondarev's programme of 'bread labour' would, as Tolstoy saw it, be a way of eliminating the inequality between rich and poor and creating brotherhood. Tolstoy compares how he and others of his class treated the poor to someone riding on the back of another man, while assuring himself and others that he was 'very sorry' for this poor man and 'wish[ed] to ease his conditions by every means in [his] power except by getting off of [the poor man's] back' (16, 99–100; 16, 81). Tolstoy calls for himself and others finally to get off the poor man's back and work for their own sustenance. He rejects counter-arguments about progress, the division of labour, and political economy.

In his own effort to do manual labour and embrace the simple life, Tolstoy took on tasks that had been performed by servants, like emptying his chamber pot and chopping wood. Tolstoy now made a programme for the fieldwork that over the years he himself, like Levin in *Anna Karenina*, had enjoyed as diversion, as exercise, or what Levin calls a 'work cure' only to have his brother point out the peasants' disapproval (3.6:261). During the winter months, Tolstoy made shoes. Visitors who had seen his handiwork quipped that they would rather read one of his novels than wear a pair of his shoes.

Tolstoy's 'bread labour' captured the imagination of his contemporaries. Many dismissed it; some wanted to try it. The English cultural critic Matthew Arnold observed that in an English village, at least, the prospect of Tolstoy working by the sweat of his brow would be greeted with 'dismay' rather than 'fraternal joy' by 'gardeners, smiths, and carpenters', who would wish him to stick to his 'articles, poetry, and nonsense', since by doing 'manual labour', he was 'taking bread from [their] mouths'. Sergii Bulgakov, a Russian theologian who had gone through a Marxist phase, praised Tolstoy's *What Then Must We Do?* for the 'vital truth' of the problem it articulates, while noting that the solutions Tolstoy offered were inadequate in part because his understanding of political economy was crude and false.

Tolstoy's (and Bondarev's) concept of 'bread labour' found an advocate in Gandhi. Manual labour was a key component in his vision and programme for a simple way of life, founded in love. While in South Africa in 1910, Gandhi established a commune called 'Tolstoy Farm' where 'bread labour' was put into practice, along with the other principles that Gandhi promoted upon his return to India in 1915.

Jane Addams, co-founder of the Chicago settlement house known as Hull House, where she worked to better the lives of poor immigrants, read *What Then Must We Do?* and made a pilgrimage to visit Tolstoy at Yasnaya Polyana in 1896. She wanted to learn more about his programme of improving lives not simply through benevolence. She especially wanted to know if 'Tolstoy's undertaking to do his daily share of the physical labor of the world…had brought him peace!' On greeting Addams, Tolstoy chided her for the waste of fabric in her bouffant sleeves, telling her there was enough there to make a frock for a child and asking her if how she dressed was 'a barrier to the people'.

After leaving Yasnaya Polyana, Addams read everything she could by Tolstoy, and, her conscience roused, she resolved that on her return to Hull House she would do two hours a day of manual labour. 'I held fast to the belief that I should do this, through the entire journey homeward, on land and sea, until I actually arrived in Chicago when suddenly the whole scheme seemed to me as utterly preposterous as it doubtless was. The half dozen people invariably waiting to see me after breakfast, the piles of letters to be opened and answered, the demand of actual and pressing wants—were these all to be pushed aside and asked to wait while I saved my soul by two hours' work at baking bread?'

Although Addams's approach to social justice differed from Tolstoy's, she championed him and his work. In her introduction to an English translation of *What Then Must We Do?*, Addams praises it for 'mak[ing] complacency impossible'. Tolstoy may have struck her as having been overly concerned with 'personal righteousness', but she recognized that he was sincere in his attempts to live a righteous life. Tolstoy never solved the problems he set forth and thus (to his credit) 'never appeared as a triumphant man'. Addams admired his simplicity and his sincerity and how throughout his life he 'would not pretend and, above all, he would not deceive himself, nor his readers' (p. xiii). Tolstoy remained one of her heroes. He was represented on a mural at Hull House, as is Abraham Lincoln. (Both are doing physical labour: Tolstoy ploughs the fields and Lincoln steers a flatboat on the Mississippi.)

In a time of famine

In 1891, severe famine hit Russia. Nikolai Leskov, a fellow writer, remembering that Tolstoy had been active in famine relief in the Samara province in 1873, appealed to Tolstoy to help. Tolstoy replied that just providing money and aid would not get at the heart of the problem. The only long-term solution he saw to the problem of hunger was a radical reordering of Russian society: brotherly love was to replace the existing order, rooted as it was in violence and in the isolation of the rich from the poor.

After writing this letter to Leskov, which ended up printed in newspapers, Tolstoy visited sites hard hit by the famine. Then, together with his wife and other family members, Tolstoy went into action with relief efforts, publicizing the need to raise funds, gathering provisions, and organizing soup kitchens run by local peasants (Figure 6).

As was typical for him, Tolstoy had mixed feelings about his involvement. He expressed doubts: 'it isn't for me to feed those by whom I'm fed.' He was just returning to the peasants who worked the land what he and others 'had stolen'. But he also declared this

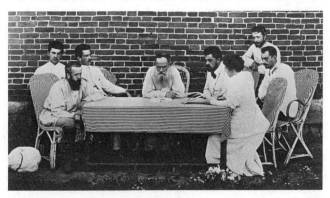

6. Tolstoy and famine relief workers in 1891.

period to have been one of the more 'happy' ones of his life because he had the sense of being engaged in a meaningful and urgent struggle against disaster. Tolstoy's ability to make things happen so awed the writer Anton Chekhov that he declared him to be some kind of 'Jupiter'.

Resurrection on the home front

Late in 1899, Tolstoy finished the novel *Resurrection*. It was first published serially, with illustrations by Leonid Pasternak, the writer Boris Pasternak's father, in an inexpensive popular weekly, with a circulation that was far greater than that of the journal that had printed his earlier novels. Meanwhile, it was also published abroad (uncensored) in Russian, as well as in translations. The royalties helped finance the move of the Dukhobors, a group of Russian sectarians persecuted by the Russian authorities, to Canada.

Tolstoy's *Resurrection* was not popular with Tolstoy's wife Sophia, who had over the years been instrumental in Tolstoy's work. (She laboured to copy his novels by hand and took an active interest in their composition and publication.) Sophia's diary gives insight into how Tolstoy's attempts to act on his convictions affected his family. Her concerns about the novel reflect points of contention in a marriage that has been subjected to a great deal of scrutiny from the public.

Sophia observed that the Dukhobors' gain (from the royalties) was a loss for the Tolstoy children, who had not been trained to earn their own money. She also questioned his choice to support the Dukhobors, rather than another, to her mind worthier, cause, such as starving peasants. She went on to note: 'But Lev Nikolaevich has dedicated his *entire* life to people and causes that are alien to me whereas I have given my *entire life to my family*.'

The content of *Resurrection* also disturbed Sophia. Like many others, she was scandalized by Tolstoy's description of the Russian

Orthodox liturgy (see Chapter 5, 'The religion of Jesus, cleansed of dogma and mysticism'). But she also objected to how her husband, 'an old man of seventy', described 'with such extraordinary gusto' the sex between the hero and the maid he seduced and abandoned. (She understood that he was fictionalizing his own past experience.) And she complained that while Tolstoy effectively describes 'moral transformations' in his books, he 'never actually achieves them in his life'.

Nekhlyudov, the hero of *Resurrection*, has struck some readers as unappealing because he is too consumed with expiating his own guilt and incapable of real compassion or love. Other readers give him credit for at least making the leap from self-involvement and privilege to awareness and outrage at the injustice around him. Readers often praise Tolstoy's skill at exposing (and railing against) injustice and hypocrisy, even if they go on to complain about Tolstoy's preachiness and didacticism. Chekhov, too, disliked how the novel lapses into gospel rhetoric instead of offering a programme for future action. But Chekhov still considered the novel 'a remarkable work of art'.

The ethics of diet at home and beyond

Tolstoy became a vegetarian and in 1892 wrote a searing description of a trip to a slaughterhouse called 'The First Step', which appeared as the introduction to Englishman Howard Williams's anthology of humanist writing on vegetarianism called *The Ethics of Diet*. Tolstoy regarded ceasing to eat meat as the first step toward a moral life. But Tolstoy was concerned, more generally, with 'the ethics of diet' and made a programme of eating abstemiously and simply. He also gave up smoking and drinking.

As with Tolstoy's later causes and convictions, intimations of his 'ethics of diet' are to be found in his earlier life and fiction. Almost thirty years earlier, in 1865, Tolstoy had expressed qualms about having 'pink radishes on our table, yellow butter, and soft, well-baked bread on a clean table-cloth', when 'elsewhere the evil devil famine is already at work, covering the fields with goose-foot, causing cracks to appear in the dried-up earth, chafing the calloused heels of the peasants and their women, cracking the hooves of the cattle and penetrating everywhere and causing such havoc to everyone'. Even as Tolstoy celebrated his family happiness in the early days of his marriage, the misery of those who put food on his table pricked his social conscience. Often, in his fiction, what someone eats reveals their character or their mood. In *Anna Karenina*, for example, the hedonist Oblonsky gorges on oysters and Anna's lover Vronsky eats beefsteak for breakfast, whereas Levin embraces simpler fare at home on his estate.

Later in life, Tolstoy complained, in his diary and out loud at family meals, about his family 'gorging' themselves with food they had not worked to prepare while others laboured and went hungry. His wife continued to provide the usual fare, thus leaving individual family members and guests to eat as they saw fit. Visitors to Yasnaya Polyana would often comment on Tolstoy eating his 'buckwheat mush'. Memoirs about Tolstoy's family life reveal that the table divided into two camps, with food choices often reflecting whether a given family member sided with Tolstoy or Sophia on this and other matters.

Tolstoy continued to struggle to find the right way to live. Representative on this front is a short diary entry from 1908 in which Tolstoy responds to a comment made by his wife about how he was preaching a simple life—and eating asparagus. Tolstoy wrote: 'she's right about the asparagus.' Tolstoy then wrote that he should 'learn how to live' (56:173). Learning how to live and what to do was for him a lifelong process. He never gave up.

Chapter 7
Tolstoy's art and devices

Tolstoy attempts to answer the question 'What is art?' in a late treatise by that name (1897). He uses the metaphor of 'infection' to describe what art—whether music, visual art, theatre, literature—does to the listener, viewer, audience, and reader. This late treatise is but one stage in Tolstoy's quest to understand art and its role in life. He had discussed these questions with his peasant pupils in school at Yasnaya Polyana and had proudly reported their views in his pedagogical writings. In his fiction he had drawn attention to how art works on the human spirit. Thus, for example, in *Childhood*, as the hero Nikolai listens to his mother play Beethoven's 'Sonata pathétique', he basks in emotion and remarks on how music makes you feel as though you are recollecting something that never happened. In *Anna Karenina*, the painter Mikhailov can only paint the Christ that is in his soul (5:12, 477). As Tolstoy understood it, he too as a writer was revealing what was in his soul.

One of the pervasive myths about Tolstoy's fiction is that he wrote 'the way the world would write if it could write by itself'. (This formulation belongs to Isaac Babel, himself a great stylist.) The lifelike quality of Tolstoy's art does not get lost in translation. Matthew Arnold, an early English critic of *War and Peace*, similarly commented on it being not 'a work of art', but 'a piece of life'. In criticism of Tolstoy's work, many follow Arnold in suggesting that Tolstoy's realism was at the expense of artistry or form. Henry James asked of *War and Peace*, 'but what do such large loose baggy monsters, with their queer elements of the accidental and the arbitrary, artistically *mean*?' Those features James took to be artless, accidental, and arbitrary are the essence of Tolstoy's art. Tolstoy uses a variety of techniques to 'infect' the readers of his fiction with what was in his soul. And these same techniques also serve in his non-fiction.

Tolstoyan realism

Tolstoy is celebrated for his seemingly faithful rendering of Russian reality. According to Dostoevsky, whose own realism is often saddled with the epithet 'fantastic', Tolstoy was the only Russian writer able to depict that reality down 'to the most minute detail'. Although he was interested in big questions about how people live, love, and die, Tolstoy also delighted in depicting the environment in which this happens. Thus, borrowing from his own world, Tolstoy gives a lot of realistic detail. The technique might seem to resemble what Roland Barthes called the 'reality effect'—that is, detail is there merely to signal the verisimilitude associated with realism but is otherwise not meaningful. However, in Tolstoy's work, as Richard Gustafson has argued, the real world is deeply meaningful. Seemingly random details often have deep significance.

At work beneath the surface of *Anna Karenina* is what Tolstoy called an 'endless labyrinth of linkages' that run through the novel connecting seemingly inconsequential realistic details into patterns of meaning. For example, on the first day of the action, Dolly neglects her maternal duties and takes to her bed, after finding out her husband Stiva had been unfaithful to her with the French governess. When Dolly gets up, her first act is to order milk for the children. This is not the only time Dolly's children will go without fresh milk. In Part 3, when Dolly is in the country with her children and the dairy cows fail to produce milk, it is not just a random mishap. Rather, this is the result of her adulterous husband's neglect. Put together, these banal details about the milk supply show how adultery affects the children in their daily life. Meanwhile, Levin nurtures his milk cows in ways that suggest he will be a loving husband, devoted to the care of his young. Later in the novel, when Anna gives birth to Vronsky's child, the baby wails because the wet nurse has no milk. And as the novel ends, Kitty is blissfully nursing Levin's son. The pattern Tolstoy sets up here is typical of his special mode of realism, in which contrary to what Barthes says, meaning is hidden everywhere. This is what makes reading Tolstoy's seemingly artless realism so rewarding.

As Dmitry Merezhkovsky saw it, 'there is simply no writer equal to Tolstoy in depicting the human body'. Tolstoy is a 'seer of the flesh' while Dostoevsky is a 'seer of the spirit'. When compared to Victorian novelists writing at the same time, Tolstoy does much more with the flesh. Tolstoy is often praised for his childbirth scenes, notably the one that tracks Levin as Kitty gives birth in *Anna Karenina*.

Tolstoy has also been accused of excessive 'naturalism', that is, for his excessive interest in human bodies. For example, the epilogue of *War and Peace* dwells on the transformation of Natasha, now married and the mother of four, into nothing but a maternal body, whose face is bereft of its former animation and whose soul is said to be not even 'visible' (Epilogue 1:10, 1242). Tolstoy's view of motherhood as the end-all and be-all of women's existence has disappointed and infuriated many readers. Still, his respect for motherhood was genuine. In *War and Peace*, he presents it as much more meaningful than the struggle for glory on the battlefield or for power in the empire.

But Tolstoy goes further with his naturalistic portrait of Natasha as mother: she is reported 'strid[ing] in', 'dishevelled in her dressing gown', in order 'with a joyful face to show a yellow instead of a green stain on baby's napkin' (Epilogue 1:10, 1244–5). For many, this detail is simply too much. Yet, in the context of *War and Peace*, this yellow-stained diaper is the emblem of her baby Petya's triumph over an illness that put him 'at death's door'. Tolstoy thus reminds us one final time—in bodily detail—that while death on the battlefield is the stuff of epic or tragedy, human beings battle for life in less dramatic, epic, and lyrical ways at home. We all live in the shadow of death (see Chapter 4).

In a habit that recalls the epithets used by Homer and other epic poets, Tolstoy repeats a particular physical detail, usually having to do with a body part, in reference to a given character. While Tolstoy sometimes uses these epithets to bring the characters to life, by making us aware of their bodies or other qualities, he often goes to extremes with this device. In *War and Peace*, as mentions of the breasts and shoulders of Hélène Kuragina accrue, the detail becomes grotesque and absurd. We're told that Hélène's breasts 'had always seemed like *marble* to Pierre', until they don't and Pierre ends up married to her (1.3:1, 219). Soon enough, Pierre, in a fury, threatens to kill Hélène, seizes a *marble* slab, brandishes it at her, but, feeling 'the fascination and delight of frenzy', he flings down the marble slab, which breaks (2.1:7, 343). Thus ends their conjugal life. As Tolstoy reinserts the marble, first conjured up in a simile, into the action, he employs another device that recurs in his work: an often eerie synergy between the real world he describes and the figurative world he creates through simile.

When, early in *War and Peace*, Andrei Bolkonsky comes in, 'rubbing his small white hands', and then proceeds to express his admiration for how Napoleon Bonaparte set a goal and then stopped at nothing to achieve it, Tolstoy signals an affinity between Andrei and Napoleon. (Tolstoy will refer to Napoleon's white hands when he comes on the scene later.) Tolstoy also imparts this physical attribute to Mikhail Speransky, an important adviser to the tsar. Tolstoy presents Speransky as a Russian stand-in for Napoleon. By merit and through ambition, Speransky, too, has risen from humble origins to power. And, a few sentences after his white hands are mentioned, Speransky is reported to have 'more than once met and talked with Napoleon' during the peace negotiations at Erfurt (2.3:5, 458). He then set about instituting Napoleonic reforms in Russia. Speransky and his work fascinate Andrei when, bored of life as an estate owner, widower, and father, he comes to Petersburg. Will Andrei, with 'small white hands' of his own, ever outgrow his tendency to admire and imitate these seemingly powerful men? Tolstoy prompts this question each time he mentions those hands.

Defamiliarization, or 'looking at things afresh'

In his 1917 essay 'Art as Technique' (sometimes translated 'Art as Device'), the Russian critic Viktor Shklovsky heralded Tolstoy as a master, although not the sole practitioner, of an artistic technique that he called defamiliarization. The technique consists of de-automatizing perception by presenting what is already familiar to the reader in a new way that makes it seem unfamiliar and strange. Rather than naming something, the artist will describe it.

Before it was christened 'defamiliarization', Tolstoy's technique had already drawn attention. In *Tolstoy and his Message* (1904), Ernest Crosby, an American follower of Tolstoy, took special note of Tolstoy's 'habit of looking at things afresh as if no one had ever considered them before'. The Russian literary critic Vinokenty Veresaev, writing in 1911, described what he saw as 'an extremely unique device' at work in Tolstoy's writings: 'it is as if an attentive, all-noticing child looked at a phenomenon and described it, not according to convention, but *simply the way it is*, such that all the habitual, hypnotizing conventions fall away from the phenomenon so that it appears in all its bare absurdity.'

The examples that Veresaev cites are among those often cited as classic examples of defamiliarization, such as the description of the opera that Natasha attends in *War and Peace*:

> In the second act there were pictures representing tombstones, and there was a round hole in the canvas to represent the moon, shades were raised over the footlights...Many people appeared from the right and left wearing black cloaks and holding things like daggers in their hands. They began waving their arms. Then some other people ran in and began dragging away the maiden who had been in white and was now in light blue. They did not drag her away at once, but sang with her for a long time and then at last dragged her off and behind the scenes something metallic was struck three times, and everyone went down on their knees and sang a prayer.
>
> (2.5:9, 604)

This technique of defamiliarizing lends itself quite naturally to the critique of culture and convention that is embedded in Tolstoy's fiction and made overt in his non-fiction. Through defamiliarization, Tolstoy attacks assumptions taken as axiomatic. He subjects all to analysis and takes nothing on faith.

Depicting inner life

When Tolstoy first broke into print with *Childhood* and the Sevastopol tales, Russian reviewers noticed something special in the way Tolstoy depicted the inner life of his characters. He even caught, in the words of Dmitry Pisarev, 'the mysterious, unclear movements of the soul that have not reached consciousness and are not completely understood even by the person who experiences them'. As his fiction became more widely known outside of Russia in the early 20th century, Tolstoy's powers for rendering consciousness continued to astound. Virginia Woolf wrote, 'Tolstoy seems able to read the minds of different people as certainly as we count the buttons on their coats.' Although Tolstoy gravitates to the interiority of some characters more than others, he gives us at least fleeting access to a large number of different consciousnesses. For Tolstoy, a glimpse is often enough to reveal a whole soul.

Throughout his career, Tolstoy developed his techniques for presenting consciousness, moving from rendering what goes on in the mind of a young officer facing his first bombardment at Sevastopol, to what is often hailed as the prototype of 'stream of consciousness' (a technique dear to Woolf and fellow Modernists) in Anna Karenina's final moments. Tolstoy moves in and out of Anna's consciousness in the last four chapters of Part 7, capturing those mysterious movements of her soul as she becomes more and more unstrung. In this respect, they recall her disjointed ramblings out loud as she lay dying after giving birth in Part 4. Those ravings, which contained more meaning and more truth than her normal speech, brought Vronsky, Karenin, and herself together in love and forgiveness in the face of death.

In Part 7, as she rides by carriage through the streets of Moscow and later through its environs by train, Anna reflects on her love and loneliness and reacts to life around her. Thus, the sound of church bells ringing triggers this:

> Everything is vile. They're ringing for vespers, and how diligently the merchant is crossing himself—as if he were afraid of dropping something. What is the point of these churches, this bell-ringing, and these lies? Just to hide the fact that we all hate each other, like these cabbies who are swearing at each other so violently.

> (7:29, 763)

At this point, after she failed to find comfort from Dolly, Anna is especially desperate, bitter, and alone. She examines her earthly attachments—subjecting them in flashes to the kind of ruthless analysis that Tolstoy conducts in a more orderly fashion as he narrates. Anna observes that her love for Vronsky was becoming 'more passionate and selfish'. Laughing schoolboys remind her of her own son, whom she had longed for. But now she thinks to herself how she was 'moved by her own tenderness' for him, but, really, she 'exchanged him for another love', that is, her love for Vronsky. While she 'was satisfied with that love', she didn't miss her son. Tolstoy shows the 'mysterious movements' of Anna's soul as a process.

Tolstoy uses various techniques for reading minds and revealing their contents. Sometimes, he quotes what characters think to themselves, leaving those thoughts in the first person and encasing them with quotation marks. At other points, he reports on a character's thoughts, reading his or her mind from his own point of view. But he also often uses a technique known as 'free indirect discourse' and will slip in words that seem to be taken directly from a character's thoughts without putting them in quotation marks.

For example, in *Hadji Murat*, when Tsar Nicholas I arrives at church, he is greeted with all sorts of praise. Then Tolstoy writes, without prefacing it with any indications that this is what was going on in Nicholas's mind: 'All this was as it should be because the happiness and the welfare of the whole world depended on him' (15, 421). Despite being presented in a neutral way, the words clearly represent Nicholas's own view of it all. The benighted priests and Nicholas's supporters may share this point of view. But Tolstoy does not. Here, as elsewhere, Tolstoy slips in and out of the minds of his characters and depends on his readers to find their bearings.

Time and plot

Tolstoy's works give the impression of 'pieces of life' in part because they usually don't have neat beginnings, middles, and ends. As Virginia Woolf put it, as Tolstoy's stories end, 'life merely goes on'. They do not 'shut with a snap' like conventional ones. Plot, as such, is downplayed: 'It is by their continuous vein of thought that we remember them, rather than by any incident.' Features that Woolf recognized in Tolstoy inspired her and other novelists, including James Joyce and William Faulkner, as they created new Modernist novel forms in the 20th century.

Tolstoy consciously and wilfully deviated from conventions of genre and expectations about unity, form, and plot. In a draft of a foreword to the first part of *War and Peace*, Tolstoy declared that he was not writing the kind of conventional novel culminating in 'a happy or unhappy denouement'—like marriage or death—that would 'destroy the interest of the narrative'. The interest of *his* narratives transcends these conventional endings. Tolstoy seemed to foresee the accusations of artlessness that would later be made against him. But Tolstoy was determined to 'be true to [his] own practices and [his] own powers' instead of following the norms of the novel.

Tolstoy's desire to capture human experience in its natural rhythms is reflected in his early habit of naming his works after units of time, such as mornings and years. Thus, when the first part of *War and Peace* was conceived and published, it was called simply 'The Year 1805'. Tolstoy was following what was already a pattern for him. For example, his first attempt at fiction was called 'A History of Yesterday' and his first attempt at a novel was the trilogy *Childhood, Boyhood, Youth*. What was to be the final part was published in aborted form as 'Landowner's Morning'. And the titles of his early war stories, 'Sevastopol in December', 'Sevastopol in May', and 'Sevastopol in August, 1855', all favour time over plot.

Instead of providing a chronicle of a given time period, Tolstoy describes selected moments that capture its essence. Thus, in *Childhood, Boyhood, Youth*, Tolstoy avoids the more continuous sequential plot of Dickens's *David Copperfield* (1850), a novel that in so many respects was one of his key inspirations. Dickens begins with a chapter called 'I Was Born' and carries on to the novel's denouement in (re)marriage. In contrast, Tolstoy's

Childhood focuses on three particular days, a few months apart, starting on the third day after the hero's tenth birthday. Each registers an emotional landmark in his becoming a motherless child. *Childhood* ends with his mother's death.

The Sevastopol tales, which followed *Childhood*, had the immediacy of real-life dispatches from the front, like those of William Russell that brought the Crimean War home to the readers of the London *Times*. But Tolstoy did not really chronicle events. Rather, as they move through the calendar, the tales acquaint us with the changing moods, from resolve to despair, with sermonic and lyrical patches that ask the eternal questions about how to live with the 'angel of death hover[ing] over' and about the vanity of human affairs.

In these tales, Tolstoy often refers to time, reminding his readers of the rhythms of the sun (also) rising and setting—on the Russians and on their enemies alike. These natural rhythms of day and night affect the bodies and souls of Tolstoy's people. Tolstoy's fiction also explores the cognitive dissonance that arises between the cyclical time in nature and the linear time of human life. Thus, moods are tied to the seasons, but also to human affairs: as the siege wears on and conditions worsen, a sense of futility takes over. The last tale ends in defeat in August 1855. Continuing this pattern, in Tolstoy's major novels, Andrei Bolkonsky and Konstantin Levin, for a while at least, forget that their days are numbered, feel rejuvenated by springtime, and take action (*War and Peace*, 2.3:3, 452; *Anna Karenina*, 2:13,154).

In 1853, Tolstoy praised himself for having adopted 'from the very start' 'the style of writing in little chapters ... express[ing] only one thought or only one feeling' (46:217). (At this point, only his *Childhood* and 'The Raid' had been published.) Tolstoy continued to use these 'little chapters' in creative ways. In fact, these 'little chapters' were essential to his way of defying conventional modes of narrating and of giving the impression of capturing real experience. For example, in 'Sevastopol in May', the little chapters divide narrative interest: they allow Tolstoy to weave in more characters, shift location, narrate simultaneous events occurring in different parts of the besieged city, and give multiple perspectives on the same event. Tolstoy does not package war into a neat story that imposes order on chaos. Instead, he conveys a distinct message or mood in each little chapter. The reader then pieces together a meaning from these little chapters—while wondering at the contradictions and the complexity of what is set forth. Tolstoy's technique of 'little chapters' adapted beautifully to his multiplot novels.

Simile and the power of comparison

George Steiner has suggested that whereas Dostoevsky's novels recall tragedies, Tolstoy's recall epics. One device Tolstoy borrows from the epic is the simile, a comparison, often long, that (in English) usually begins with 'like' or 'as'. This device marks a given point in the action, then carries the focus elsewhere to the realm of the comparison, and brings that elsewhere to bear on the point in the action that prompted the simile. A simile involves an associative or intuitive leap. Homer used similes to draw the different realms of his epic universe together and to include all aspects of life in it. Tolstoy would do the same.

In *War and Peace*, similes often compare the realm of war to that of peace, or vice versa. When Liza Bolkonskaya springs into action as a matchmaker when a suitor for her unmarried sister-in-law arrives on the scene, the novel likens her to 'an old war-horse that hears the trumpet' as she 'prepared for the familiar gallop of coquetry' (1.3:4, 241). This is Tolstoy's playful way of indicating that courtship is to women what battle is to men—or to horses trained for warfare. Yet, in Tolstoy's world, as in Homer's, if you linger over a simile, it opens up a rat's nest of questions. That Ippolit Kuragin is so ill suited to Marya Bolkonskaya reveals the absurdity of it all. If courtship practices are this ridiculous, then what about the battle that the poor old horse serves in?

Tolstoy also often compared humans to animals or to other aspects of the natural world. A simile that recalls one that Virgil used for Carthage in the *Aeneid* likens Moscow, emptied out as Napoleon arrives, to a queenless beehive—and develops the analogy for a whole chapter (3.3:20, 938–40). At other points, the novel compares the troops marching to the forces at play in the natural world, in order to prepare the reader for Tolstoy's theorizing about human agency and God's role in the universe. The simile invites us to wonder: do the same forces govern both the natural and the human realms?

In his *Lectures on Russian Literature*, Vladimir Nabokov remarked on a whole class of Tolstoyan similes that follows the formula: someone felt 'like a person who …'. Thus, in *Anna Karenina*, Karenin, on discovering the emotional distance that has arisen between him and Anna as a result of her passion for Vronsky, experiences 'a sensation' 'like that which might be experienced by someone who has returned home and found his house locked' (2:9, 148). These similes make the particular experience of a character accessible and suggest that this experience reveals something about human experience.

Similes are a special case of Tolstoy's general fascination with comparisons. Within the action of his works, Tolstoy shows his characters engaging in the mental act of making comparisons. For example, *Anna Karenina* depicts Kitty comparing Levin and Vronsky, her two suitors, imagining each on his own and then 'both together' (1:13; 49). *Hadji Murat* describes Tsar Nicholas thinking about the frightened look of the young woman he has just seduced, and 'now of the full, powerful shoulders of his established mistress, Nelidova', and then 'compar[ing] the two' (15, 421).

As a young man, Tolstoy had already recognized the process of making comparisons as vital to the workings of the human mind. In a notebook he kept during the spring of 1847 (as he was dropping out of Kazan University), as Tolstoy set forth a programme for self-improvement on various fronts, he identified 'five main mental faculties.' They are: 'the faculty of *conceptualization*, the faculty of *memory*, the faculty of *comparison*, the faculty of *drawing conclusions from these comparisons*, and, finally, the faculty of *putting these conclusions in order*' (46:271). From the rest of the diary entry, it's clear that Tolstoy was especially interested in comparisons. Mental operations for him were not just on a linear axis, with one thing connecting directly to another. He was aware that the human mind works by leaps and bounds and he wanted to harness these within his art.

Hidden symmetries

The young Tolstoy also composed a 'philosophical treatise' on symmetry, a foundational concept in aesthetics that hinges on similarity and opposition. The manuscript didn't survive. However, in *Boyhood,* the hero Nikolai is seen musing, with chalk in hand, about symmetry, wondering whether it is an inborn feeling, and wanting to know if human life is governed by it. When Tolstoy turned to writing, he made use of mental operations, aesthetic principles, and artistic devices based in comparisons, opposition, and symmetry—the concepts that he had identified and described in his philosophical and aesthetic enquiries of younger years.

On a larger scale than the similes and comparisons, Tolstoy structured scenes and sometimes entire storylines around hidden symmetries which invite readers to compare them and find meaning in their parallels or contrasts. The structure of his works often depends on what Percy Lubbock complained was nothing more than 'pictorial contrast': two or more plots or scenes that do not intersect through dramatic action but require the reader to compare them.

As the title *War and Peace* suggests, Tolstoy was fascinated with binary oppositions. From that title on, he employs different artistic means of prompting the reader to compare and contrast what appear to be parallel but opposed phenomena, such as war and peace, battle and courtship, French and Russian, friend and foe, male and female, lord and master, human and animal, and a host of others. He engages us in a process of pondering these oppositions. What do they reveal about the way we think and the way we live?

In *War and Peace*, Tolstoy presents Kutuzov, who leads the Russian forces, as an analogue and opposite to Napoleon, who has recently crowned himself emperor of France. In depicting Kutuzov, Tolstoy was more concerned with sharpening the contrast with Napoleon than with sticking to the facts. This contrast becomes explicit when, for example, before the Battle of Borodino, Tolstoy shows each responding to a painted image: Kutuzov joins others as they prostrate themselves before an icon of the Mother of God with the Christ child in her arms (3.2:21, 819) while the next time we see Napoleon, he admires a painting of his pudgy toddler son, dubbed the 'Roi de Rome' (King of Rome), playing with a stick and ball, with the latter representing the earth and the former a sceptre, in an 'allegory' that seemed 'quite clear and very pleasing' to Napoleon (3.2:27, 836). Tolstoy created these scenes, with all their parallels and contrasts, to be understood in their own separate contexts but also to mean something more when understood as a pair.

The famous opening sentence of *Anna Karenina*—'All happy families are alike, each unhappy family is unhappy in its own way'—signals that in this novel, as in *War and Peace*, Tolstoy is interested in juxtaposing seemingly opposite phenomena and also in comparing phenomena that seem to belong to the same category (of unhappy families) to reveal differences. Close study of

Anna Karenina reveals a host of parallels and contrasts. Tolstoy often pairs and sometimes triples characters or situations.

Above all, *Anna Karenina* is known for how it compares and contrasts its different plotlines. Readers of *Anna Karenina* often comment on the loose connection between its plots. Indeed, in other multiplot novels, such as those of Charles Dickens or George Eliot, the plots tend to intersect and sometimes even fuse together. But Tolstoy eschewed this model. Henry James, famous for complaining about Tolstoy's loose novelistic form, was not alone—or the first. In 1886, Teddy Roosevelt reported in a letter to his sister: 'there are two entirely different stories in it; the connection between Levin's story and Anna's is of the slightest, and need not have existed at all.' What Tolstoy does with the plots of *Anna Karenina* struck readers like Roosevelt and James as making the structure of the novel seem haphazard: it made them wonder if Tolstoy's work lacked unity. But, in fact, what Tolstoy does is far from being random or artless (Figure 7).

Much as Tolstoy mined with meaning all of the seemingly lifelike random details, creating what he called 'an endless labyrinth of linkages' that binds the novel together, so too did Tolstoy design for *Anna Karenina* a hidden artistic structure. The Formalist critic Boris Eikhenbaum wrote that *Anna Karenina* was 'built on the very open and simple parallelism of two lines', connected by a dotted line. But the analogy that Tolstoy in fact had in mind was architectural. When his friend Sergei Rachinsky expressed regret that Tolstoy had kept his plots apart instead of connecting them, which would have made the novel more traditional, Tolstoy indicated that he was in fact proud of the architectonics of *Anna Karenina*: he had constructed it with care. He explained that the structure of *Anna Karenina* depended *not* on external links, such as meetings between characters of the different plots, but rather on inner connections, whether of similarity or of contrast. He explained that the linkages between plots were beneath the surface and thus 'hidden' by design.

7. Tolstoy's drawings in the manuscript of *Anna Karenina*.

Tolstoy's daring act of submerging the connections between his plots is one feature of *Anna Karenina* which was later adopted by modern novelists. Thus, for example, Virginia Woolf's *Mrs. Dalloway* tells two stories at once, that of Clarissa Dalloway, wife of a Minister of Parliament, and that of Septimus Warren Smith, a shell-shocked veteran of the Great War: the two never meet, but Woolf, like Tolstoy before her, forces the reader to ponder the interrelatedness of human lives.

Tolstoy does not make the links between the plots overt. He leaves it up to readers to work out the links between the plots and to bear in mind all the characters and all the plotlines as they read (and after they close the book). The process of reading *Anna Karenina* means reading each of its 'little chapters' on its own and as part of sequences, while also relating them to other chapters. In fact, Tolstoy requires his readers to use all their 'mental faculties'—such as the five he identified as a teenager: 'the faculty of *conceptualization*, the faculty of *memory*, the faculty of *comparison*, the faculty of *drawing conclusions from these comparisons*, and, finally, the faculty of *putting these conclusions in order*' (46:271). Thus, Tolstoy asks the reader to conceptualize what he describes at any given point in the novel and to remember and bear it in mind while continuing on, perhaps shifting from one situation to another situation, from one character to another, and then to make comparisons, draw conclusions, and attempt to put them in order.

Thus, even while we're cosy with Kitty and Levin and their loved ones at their estate in Part 8, we wonder about the tenuous state of the Oblonsky family. And, above all, we recall Anna Karenina's bitter despair as she rode through the streets of Moscow and environs at the end of Part 7, feeling that enmity rules on earth. How do these scenes compare and how do they connect?

By design, mustering all the artistic devices that make his art so glorious, Tolstoy creates a novel that, in fact, makes the reader into an Ant Brother who, from wherever that reader might be, under whatever circumstances, thinks not just about the here and now, what is immediate, but also bears in mind others, all God's children under the cope of heaven who should be united in love.

Chapter 8
Tolstoy cannot be silent

For his last thirty years, from *Confession* (1879–82) to 'I Cannot Be Silent' (1908), Tolstoy often spoke out in the first person, dispensing with the veil of fiction. These works were widely disseminated. Essays by Tolstoy appeared in newspapers around the world, as did news items about him and reports by visitors to his estate Yasnaya Polyana.

In 'I Cannot Be Silent', Tolstoy spoke out with the intention of inspiring and provoking everyone, from the tsar to readers around the globe. This felt more urgent to him as he approached death. Newspapers in Russia that published excerpts were fined. But it circulated in illegally printed copies. Abroad it appeared in a number of newspapers, such as the *New York Times*. Typical as it is of his late mode, 'I Cannot Be Silent' also shows—in an extreme and highly concentrated form—the devices, techniques, and subject matter that give Tolstoy's fiction its power. Tolstoy returned to the questions about love, death, brotherhood, and the pain of others that he had posed from the start (Figure 8).

In 'I Cannot Be Silent', Tolstoy writes that on 9 May 1908 he read in the paper that 'twenty peasants were hung for an attack, made with intent to rob, on a landed proprietor's estate in the Elisabetgrad district' (395). He had been reading about these executions day in and day out, 'not for months', 'but for years'.

8. From the *New York Times*, 19 July 1908.

Political unrest had only escalated in the years since 1902, when Tolstoy had written to the tsar—addressing him as 'Dear brother', and advising him that repressive measures would just make the situation worse. When revolution erupted in 1905, the unrest continued. Executions, once banned in Russia, had become commonplace. As Tolstoy explains, the government justified these executions on the grounds that they were necessary for the public good. Since he lived in Russia, then, these hangings were ostensibly being performed for his 'welfare'—to protect his privileged way of life.

Defamiliarizing the hanging of men

Early in 'I Cannot Be Silent' Tolstoy describes the hanging of these peasants—but he refers to them not as twenty peasants but as 'twenty of those by whose labor we live' and 'whom we deprave'. Step by step, he breaks down the procedure, also without naming it. The executioner dissolves soap in water, soaps the loops of the cords 'that they may tighten better'. Tolstoy reports that 'beside them walks a long-haired man wearing a stole and vestments made of gold or silver cloth, and with a cross in his hand...'. This 'long-haired man, addressing those whom other people are about to strangle with cords, says something about God and Christ'.

This section ends as follows: 'And then, one after another, living men are pushed off the benches which are drawn from under their feet, and by their own weight suddenly tighten the nooses round their necks and are painfully strangled. Men, alive a minute before, become corpses dangling from a rope, at first swinging slowly and then resting motionless' (395–6). This is a classic example of Tolstoy's technique of defamiliarization. Here, Tolstoy uses it to denounce and to expose, as well as to 'prick at our conscience.' (See Chapter 7, 'Defamiliarization, or "looking at things afresh".)

Tolstoy focuses on how responsibility for these executions and other forms of state-sanctioned violence (such as that in the penal system described in *Resurrection*) is parcelled out. Those who decide on punishments do not carry them out; others are coerced into participating. Thus, because 'responsibility for these iniquities is subdivided among those who commit them', 'each may think and say that it is not he who is responsible for them' (397). Here Tolstoy returns to questions about events that occur as the aggregate of the action of a large number of people that he explored in *War and Peace*. For Tolstoy, it was not a matter of this violence being nobody's fault; it is everybody's fault. And he wants each person to take responsibility.

Remember who you are!

In 'I Cannot Be Silent', Tolstoy examines the guilt that he felt for what he calls the 'terrible deeds' and 'terrible crimes' that upheld his life: 'Strange as it seems to say that all this is done for me, and that I am a participator in these terrible deeds, I cannot but feel that there is an indubitable interdependence between my spacious room, my dinner, my clothing, my leisure, and the terrible crimes committed to get rid of those who would like to take from me what I have' (410). Tolstoy uses another of his favourite techniques, that of contrasting disparate scenes or realities and of indicating the links between them. (See Chapter 7, 'Hidden symmetries'.) In this case, he connects his comfort to the suffering of others.

That 'the atrocities committed by the revolutionaries are terrible', Tolstoy did not dispute (405). But he considers what the government was doing in response to be just as bad. These executions confirmed what he suspected as a boy, when he learned that peasants were beaten: that violence was the means used to enforce the existing order, whether on the level of estate or empire. Thus, Tolstoy declares:

> It is impossible to live so! I, at any rate, cannot and will not live so. That is why I write this and will circulate it by all means in my power both in Russia and abroad—that one of two things may happen: either that these inhuman deeds may be stopped, or that my connexion with them may be snapped and I be put in prison...or...that they may put on me, as on those twelve or twenty peasants, a shroud and a cap and may push me too off a bench, so that by my own weight I may tighten the well-soaped noose round my old throat. (411)

Here, he escalates the argument made by American writer Henry David Thoreau (whose likeness hung in Tolstoy's study) in his essay 'Civil Disobedience': 'under a government that imprisons any unjustly, the true place for a just man is also in prison.' In *Resurrection*, Tolstoy's hero recalls these words and agrees (2:29, 331).

Tolstoy still holds hope that 'these inhuman deeds' would stop. He addresses the tsar and others, saying: 'But none of you—from the Secretary of the Court to the Premier and the Tsar—who are indirect participators in the iniquities perpetrated every day, seem to feel your guilt or the shame that your participation in these horrors ought to evoke' (408). In 'I Cannot Be Silent', Tolstoy uses all his powers of description and denunciation to make them feel that guilt and shame.

But, towards the end of 'I Cannot Be Silent', Tolstoy calls for all, from the tsar, to the hangman, and to the reader, to remember that they are human beings, 'today allowed a peep into God's world, tomorrow ceasing to be', and that it was their duty to live out what is left of their lives 'in accord with the Will that sent you into this world'. And 'that Will desires only one thing': for us to love one another (411–12).

As the world prepared to pay tribute to him on his eightieth birthday, Tolstoy called for the anger and killing to stop and made a last resounding plea, in the spirit of the Ant Brothers. 'Brother people! Come to your senses, bethink yourselves, understand what you are doing! Remember who you are!' (411).

Chronology

1859	Sets up school for peasants on his estate
1860	Trip to Western Europe; at brother Nikolai's deathbed; Aksinya Bazykina, a peasant, gives birth to Tolstoy's son
1863	Marries Sophia Andreevna Behrs; she will give birth to thirteen children over twenty-five years (six will die before Tolstoy)
1863–9	At work on *War and Peace*
1869	Arzamas terror
1873	Famine relief work in Samara
1873–7	*Anna Karenina*
1877	Turn to religion
1879–84	Composes *Confession, Gospel in Brief* and a longer work on the Gospels; *What I Believe*
1881–2	Volunteers for census in Moscow; begins *What Then Must We Do?*
1883	Refuses jury duty
1886	'How Much Land Does a Man Need?' 'Death of Ivan Ilyich'
1888	Becomes vegetarian; promotes temperance; preaches sexual abstinence
1889	'The Kreutzer Sonata'
1891–3	Famine relief work
1893	*The Kingdom of God Is Within You*
1894	Gandhi reads *Kingdom of God Is Within You* in South Africa; Ernest Howard Crosby visits Yasnaya Polyana
1896	Jane Addams visits Tolstoy
1897	*What Is Art?*
1899	*Resurrection*
1900	'Need It Be So?'
1901	Excommunicated by Russian Orthodox Church
1902	Writes to tsar, addressing him as 'Dear brother'
1904	Finishes *Hadji Murat* (publ. 1912)

1904–5	Russo-Japanese War and Revolution of 1905; 'Bethink Yourselves'
1908	*I Cannot Be Silent*; 80th birthday celebrations
1909–10	Correspondence with Gandhi
1910	Tolstoy leaves home, dies of pneumonia at Astapovo; buried by the green stick back at Yasnaya Polyana

References

Chapter 1: From Ant Brothers to loving all as brothers and sisters

Tolstoy as writer, thinker, man

Hemingway wished that Turgenev had written *War and Peace* in a letter to Archibald Macleish (20 December 1925) and he declared Tolstoy the best writer on war while rejecting 'ponderous and Messianic thinking' in the introduction to his 1942 anthology *Men at War*. Mark Twain's comment about 'bring[ing] down Tolstoy' is found in his *Notebooks and Journals*, ed. Frederick Anderson (Berkeley: U California P, 1979), vol. 3, p. 240. William Dean Howells's comments were in his 'Editor's Study', *Harper's Monthly Magazine*, vol. 72 (Dec. 1885–May 1886), pp. 808–10.

Ant Brothers and the green stick

Many biographers and scholars discuss the importance of Ant Brothers and Tolstoy's yearnings for universal love; illuminating for me has been the work of Richard Gustafson on Tolstoy as 'resident and stranger' (*Leo Tolstoy: Resident and Stranger* (Princeton: Princeton UP, 1986) and of Anne Hruska on 'belonging and exclusion' in Tolstoy's novels (*Infected Families: Belonging and Exclusion in the Works of Leo Tolstoy*, dissertation, University of California, Berkeley, 2001).

Chapter 2: Tolstoy on war and on peace

In his poem '*Dulce et decorum est*' the English poet of the First World War Wilfred Owen, after describing a gas attack, declared the Roman poet Horace's lines about it being sweet and fitting to die for one's country to be 'an old lie' told 'to children ardent for some desperate glory'. On Tolstoy's early war stories in relation to his later pacifism, see Liza Knapp, 'The Development of Style and Theme in Tolstoy', in D. Orwin, ed., *The Cambridge Companion to Tolstoy* (Cambridge: Cambridge UP, 2002), pp. 159–75.

Tolstoy and his forerunners

In *Tolstoy or Dostoevsky: An Essay in the Old Criticism* (New York: Dutton, 1971), George Steiner, contrasting Dostoevsky's 'tragic world view' to Tolstoy's epic one, explores Tolstoy's ties to Homer. Steiner quotes Gorky on p. 71. The French critic cited is Alphonse Séché, *Stendhal* (Paris: Société des Éditions Louis-Michaud, [1912]), p. 110; Boris Eikhenbaum refers to these comments in *The Young Tolstoy*, trans. Garry Kern (Ann Arbor: Ardis, 1982), p. 81. For Fabrice's view of war after the battle of Waterloo, see Stendhal, *The Charterhouse of Parma*, trans. Roger Pearson (Oxford: Oxford World's Classics, 2009), p. 55. Tolstoy made his comments about Stendhal in an interview with Paul Boyer in 1901. They are cited in Paul Birukoff, *Leo Tolstoy: His Life and Work* (New York: Scribner, 1906), 1:199. Carl von Clausewitz had also used this device in his treatise *On War* (1832). In Part 1, chapter 4 'The Danger of War', Clausewitz makes readers into war tourists: 'Let us accompany a novice to the battlefield', then describes the danger as a novice would experience it. See: <https://www.clausewitz.com/readings/OnWar1873/BK1ch04.html#a>.

War as it is and the shadow of death in Sevastopol

William Russell writes of having been 'honoured with abuse for telling the truth' in *Dispatches from the Crimea* (London: Frontline, 2008), p. 163. Tolstoy's appreciation of the 'plain unsung hero' was noted by Peter Kropotkin and quoted by Aylmer Maude in *Leo Tolstoy: The First Fifty Years* (New York: Dodd, 1910), p. 133. For Walt Whitman on the hospital as the site where the 'real war' is witnessed, see his *Memoranda during the War* (Camden, NJ, 1875–6), p. 5. <https://whitmanarchive.org/published/other/memoranda.html>.

Imitation of, and war against, Napoleon in *War and Peace*

On Napoleon and the novel, see Franco Moretti, *Way of the World: The Bildungsroman in European Culture* (New York: Verso, 2000), p. 76. The Russian novel has had a complicated relation to Napoleon: the plots of some of the precursors to *War and Peace*, such as Pushkin's *Eugene Onegin*, Lermontov's *Hero of our Time*, Gogol's *Dead Souls*, have heroes that imitate and admire Napoleon (and suffer from it).

And Dostoevsky's *Crime and Punishment*, which was published serially as *War and Peace* was starting to appear, features a hero who imagined there was such a thing as 'extraordinary people', Napoleon among them, who had the right to kill in order to bring some new idea to the world. For Tolstoy's views on great men, war, and history, see Isaiah Berlin, *The Hedgehog and the Fox* (New York: Simon & Schuster, 1986 [1953]).

How to tell a true story

'How to Tell a True War Story' is the title of a war story by Tim O'Brien in *The Things They Carried* (New York: Houghton, Mifflin, 1990). Berlin discusses how accounts of battles differ from 'what really occurred' on pp. 15–16.

Chapter 3: Love

Tolstoy reported weeping at the bed of the prostitute in conversation with M. A. Shmidt, *c*.1898; see N. N. Gusev, *Lev Nikolaevich Tolstoi: Materialy k biografii s 1828 po 1855 god* (Moscow: A. N. SSSR, 1954), pp. 168–9. Lydia Ginzburg characterized Tolstoy's prose as 'autopsychological' in *On Psychological Prose*, trans. Judson Rosengrant (Princeton: Princeton University Press, 1991), p. 198. For discussion of Tolstoy's 'autopsychological prose', see Richard Gustafson, *Leo Tolstoy: Resident and Stranger* (Princeton: Princeton University Press, 1986). Freud addresses the problem of neighbourly love in *Civilization and its Discontents*, trans . James Strachey (New York: Norton, 1961), pp. 100–1.

Courtship, marriage, and family happiness in *War and Peace*

Boris Eikhenbaum discusses Tolstoy's intention to end *War and Peace* 'with all possible marriages resolving all the family conflicts and unraveling all the knots of the plot' in *Tolstoi in the Sixties*, trans. Duffield White (Ann Arbor: Ardis, 1982), pp. 147–8. For the contrast between the vitality of the Russian family and the 'system' of Napoleon and the French, see John Bayley, *Tolstoy and the Novel* (Chicago: U Chicago P, 1966), pp. 62–176.

Adultery and marriage in *Anna Karenina*

Matthew Arnold compares *Anna Karenina* to *Madame Bovary* in his 1887 essay 'Count Leo Tolstoi', reprinted in Henry Gifford, ed., *Leo Tolstoy* (Harmondsworth: Penguin, 1971), pp. 60–80. See pp. 69–70. For Emma Bovary passionately kissing the crucifix, see Gustave Flaubert, *Madame Bovary*, trans. Malcolm Bowie (Oxford: Oxford World's Classics, 2008), pp. 288–9.

Sex as scandal in 'The Kreutzer Sonata'

When a hawker went on trial in Philadelphia for selling 'The Kreutzer Sonata', the judge read the story and concluded that while it 'contains some very absurd and foolish views on marriage', and while 'it may shock our ideas of the sanctity and nobility of that relation', it was not 'obscene libel'. See: *New York Times*, 25 September 1890, 'Count Tolstoi Not Obscene'. William Stead made his claim about noble Anglo-Saxon love in *Review of Reviews*, 1890. In 'The Kreutzer Sonata', Pozdnyshev complained of the hypocrisy of the English about sexual mores: they make such a pretence of their chastity that they start to believe that they are in fact 'moral people' and 'live in a moral world' (5, 100). Chekhov comments on 'The Kreutzer Sonata' in a letter to Alexei Pleshcheev, 15 February 1890, in Gifford, ed., *Leo Tolstoy*, p. 97. For the impact on Zhivago and his friends of 'The Kreutzer Sonata', see Boris Pasternak, *Doctor Zhivago*, trans. Manya Harari and Max Hayward (New York: Pantheon, 1997), p. 40.

From sexual guilt to responsibility and resurrection

Pavel Biryukov reports on his conversation with Tolstoy about sexual guilt and discusses its impact on his fiction in ch. 8 of 'Autobiographical Elements in L. N. Tolstoi's Works', in *Tolstoi's Love Letters*, trans. S. S. Koteliansky and Virginia Woolf (Richmond: Hogarth Press, 1923).

Chapter 4: Death

Andrei's love and forgiveness in the face of death

'How does Count Tolstoy know this [what it is like to die]?' was Konstantin Leontiev's question in *The Novels of Count L. N. Tolstoy* (1890), quoted in Gifford, ed., *Leo Tolstoy*, p. 88. Mikhail Bakhtin discusses Tolstoy's 'passion' for depicting death in 'Towards a Reworking of the Dostoevsky Book' in *Problems of Dostoevsky's Poetics*, trans. Caryl Emerson (Minneapolis: U of Minnesota Press, 1984), p. 289.

Memento mori in *Anna Karenina*

For Dostoevsky's comments on how the proximity of death affects Anna, her lover, and her husband, see the excerpt from his *Diary of a*

Writer, trans. Boris Brasol (1949), as quoted in Gifford, ed.,
Leo Tolstoy, pp. 49–50. Matthew Arnold's comment is from
'Count Leo Tolstoi', also in Gifford, ed., p. 68.

Levin and death

Blaise Pascal writes of the infinite abyss that only faith will fill in
fragment #181 of the Sellier edition. See *Pensées and Other Writings*,
trans. Honor Levi (Oxford: Oxford World's Classics, 2008), pp. 51–2.

The death of Leo Tolstoy

Tolstoy's letter to his wife on his rationale for leaving home is quoted
from Paul Birukoff, *The Life of Tolstoy* (London: Cassell, 1911), p. 149.

On Tolstoy's death see William Nickell, *The Death of Tolstoy: Russia
on the Eve, Astapovo Station, 1910* (Ithaca, NY: Cornell UP, 2010).

Chapter 5: What Tolstoy believed

For the text of Turgenev's letter to Tolstoy (July 1883), see Gifford, ed.,
Leo Tolstoy, pp. 55–6.

The religion of Jesus, cleansed of dogma and mysticism

On the continuity in Tolstoy's thought, see Richard Gustafson,
Leo Tolstoy, Resident and Stranger (Princeton: Princeton UP, 1986)
and Inessa Medzhibovskaya, *Tolstoy and the Religious Culture of his
Time: A Biography of a Long Conversion* (Lanham, Md: Lexington
Books, 2009). Sophia Tolstoy reacted to her husband's description of
the Eucharist in *Resurrection* in her diary on 26 January 1899. I cite
from *Diaries of Sophia Tolstoy*, trans. Cathy Porter (New York:
Random House, 1985), p. 371. The excerpts she quotes are perfect
examples of the device Shklovsky called 'defamiliarization'. (See
Chapter 7.)

Russian Orthodox doctrine and practice at odds
with Jesus's teaching

I cite the translation of Tolstoy's diary entry of 22 May 1878 from
Aylmer Maude's *The Life of Tolstoy: Later Years* (New York: Dodd
Mead, 1911), p. 4.

Tolstoy's gospel

For discussion of Tolstoy's Jesus, see Hugh McLean, 'Tolstoy's Jesus', in
In Quest of Tolstoy (Brighton, Mass.: Academic Studies Press, 2008),

pp. 117–42. McLean cites Tolstoy's remark about not caring whether Jesus was resurrected, as reported by I. M. Ivakin, on pp. 122–3. (See also 24:980.) G. K. Chesterton complained about Tolstoy's 'cutting up' of Jesus's teaching in: 'Tolstoy and the Cult of Simplicity', in *Varied Types* (1903), p. 142. Chesterton argues that Tolstoy destroyed what he considered to be the best feature of Jesus's teaching: its 'absolute spontaneity'. Chesterton still considered Tolstoy's 'Christianity' to be 'one of the most thrilling and dramatic incidents in our modern civilization'. Ernest Howard Crosby comments on Tolstoy's reworking of the gospel in *Tolstoy and his Message* (London: Arthur C. Fifield/ Simple Life Press, 1904), p. 26.

'But who is my neighbour?'

Tolstoy warns against 'ratiocination' about who one's neighbour is in his *Four Gospels Harmonized* (24:666). Sophia Tolstoy's observation about Tolstoy acquiring 'millions of people' as brothers is from: *Diaries,* trans. Cathy Porter (New York: Random House, 1985), p. 854 (translated emended).

Non-violence in Gethsemane, at Yasnaya Polyana, and beyond

Ernest Howard Crosby reports on 'the jam and the stick' in *Tolstoy as Schoolmaster* (London: Arthur Fifield, Simple Life Press, 1904), pp. 67–70.

The impact of Tolstoy's religious works

On the impact on Gandhi of Tolstoy's *The Kingdom of God*, see: Joseph Lelyveld, *Great Soul: Mahatma Gandhi and his Struggle with India* (New York: Vintage, 2012), p. 36. John Coleman Kenworthy's comment on Tolstoy's impact in England is from: *Tolstoy: His Life and Works* (London; Walter Scott Publishing Company, 1902), pp. 39–40. On the activities of Tolstoy's disciples, see Charlotte Alston, *Tolstoy and his Disciples: The History of a Radical International Movement* (London: I. B. Tauris, 2014). On Tolstoy's impact on Wittgenstein, see Irina Paperno, *'Who, What Am I?' Tolstoy Struggles to Narrate the Self* (Ithaca, NY: Cornell University Press, 2014), pp. 78–9 and Ray Monks, *Ludwig Wittgenstein: The Duty of Genius* (New York: Macmillan, 1990).

Chapter 6: What then must we do?

In 'Need It Be So?', 'What Then Must We Do?', and other works, Tolstoy tasks his reader with the same reckoning that Susan Sontag calls for in *Regarding the Pain of Others* (New York: Farrar, Straus, & Giroux, 2004): she is not after sympathy, which 'proclaims our innocence as well as our impotence', but 'reflection on how our privileges are located on the same map as [the] suffering [of others], and may—in ways we might prefer not to imagine—be linked to their suffering, as the wealth of some may imply the destitution of others'.

Who should own land?

For James Joyce's praise of 'How Much Land Does a Man Need', see *Selected Letters*, ed. Richard Ellman (New York: Viking, 1975), pp. 372–3.

For George Orwell on Tolstoy, see: 'Lear, Tolstoy, and the Fool', *The Orwell Reader: Fiction, Essays, and Reportage* (New York: Harcourt, 1984), pp. 300–14.

Tolstoy and the Moscow poor

Aylmer Maude calls *What Then Must We Do?* Tolstoy's most 'soul-stirring' work. See *The Life of Tolstoy: The Later Years* (New York: Dodd, 1911), pp. 100–1. On Siutaev and Tolstoy, see pp. 67–75 of N. N. Gusev, *Lev Nikolaevich Tolstoi: Materialy k biografii s 1881 po 1885 god* (Moscow: Nauka, 1970).

Tolstoy on labour and the simple life

In *What Then Must We Do?* Tolstoy praised Bondarev and Siutaev together, writing: 'In my whole life two Russian thinkers have had a great moral influence on me, enriched my thought, and cleared up my outlook on life. These men were not Russian poets, or learned men, or preachers—they were remarkable men who are still living, both of them peasants' (38, 320). Matthew Arnold comments on Tolstoy's manual labour in: 'Count Leo Tolstoi', *Essays in Criticism* (1888), reprinted in Gifford, ed., *Leo Tolstoy*, p. 80. Sergii Bulgakov responds to *What Then Must We Do?* in S. N. Bulgakov, 'Prostota i oproshchenie', *O religii L'va Tolstogo. Sbornik statei* (Paris: YMCA, 1978; reprint of Moscow, 1912 edition), p. 114.

On Gandhi and Tolstoy: see Martin Green, *Tolstoy and Gandhi: Men of Peace* (New York: Harper Collins, 1999). See also Steven G. Marks, *How Russia Shaped the Modern World: From Art to Anti-Semitism, Ballet to Bolshevism* (Princeton: Princeton UP, 2003), ch. 4, pp. 102–39. Marks notes that Tolstoy indirectly, especially through Gandhi, influenced Martin Luther King, Jr and others active in the Civil Rights movement in the USA.

My source on Addams and Tolstoy is: James Cracraft, *Two Shining Souls: Jane Addams, Leo Tolstoy, and the Quest for Global Peace* (Lanham, Md: Lexington Books, 2012). Jane Addams described her interest in and visit to Tolstoy in a chapter titled 'Tolstoyism', pp. 259–80 of *Twenty Years at Hull House* (New York: Macmillan, 1911), and she commented further in other works, including her introduction to an English translation of *What Then Must We Do?*

In a time of famine

Tolstoy writes that 'it's not for me to feed those by whom I'm fed' in a letter to I. B. Feinerman (23 November 1891). See *Letters of Tolstoy*, trans. R. F. Christian, 2:489. Tolstoy writes in positive terms about his famine relief work to his cousin A. A. Tolstaia on 8 December 1891 (66:106–7). Chekhov declares Tolstoy to be a 'Jupiter' who got things done to help the victims of famine in a letter to A. S. Suvorin of 11 December 1891.

Resurrection on the home front

Tolstoy had not been collecting any royalties on other works written since 1881 and he had turned over the copyright to his pre-1881 works to his wife. The passages from Sophia Tolstoy's diaries on *Resurrection* are from 13 September 1898. I cite from *Diaries of Sophia Tolstoy*, trans. Cathy Porter (New York: Random House, 1985), pp. 341–2. Chekhov's comment about *Resurrection* is quoted by Hugh McLean, '*Resurrection*', in Donna Tussing Orwin, ed., *The Cambridge Companion to Tolstoy* (Cambridge: Cambridge University Press, 2002), p. 110.

The ethics of diet at home and beyond

Tolstoy wrote of the plenty on his table while famine loomed elsewhere in a letter to his friend and neighbour the poet Afanasy Fet, on 16 May 1865. I quote from *Letters*, trans. Christian, 1:95.

Chapter 7: Tolstoy's art and devices

The comments about Tolstoy's 'lifelike' writing are from: Isaac Babel, 'Babel Answers Questions about his Work: An Interview of 28 September, 1937'; Matthew Arnold, 'Count Leo Tolstoi', *Essays in Criticism*; Henry James, 'Preface to *The Tragic Muse*', as reprinted in Gifford, ed., *Leo Tolstoy*, p. 203, p. 80, and p. 104.

Tolstoyan realism

Dostoevsky commented on Tolstoy's grip on reality in a letter to Kh. D. Alchevskaia, of 9 April 1876. Barthes describes 'the reality effect' in an essay by that name in *The Rustle of Language*, trans. Richard Howard (Berkeley: U of California P, 1989), pp. 141–8. Richard Gustafson explores what he calls Tolstoy's 'emblematic realism' in *Resident and Stranger: A Study in Fiction and Theology* (Princeton: Princeton UP, 1986), see especially 'The Poetics of Emblematic Realism', pp. 202–13. Tolstoy refers to this 'hidden labyrinth of linkages' in a letter to N. N. Strakhov of 23 April 1876, in Gifford, ed., *Leo Tolstoy*, p. 48. For discussion see my *Anna Karenina and Others: Tolstoy's Labyrinth of Plots* (Madison: U of Wisconsin P, 2016). Dmitry Merezhkovsky presents Tolstoy as 'seer of the flesh' in *Tolstoi as Man and Artist* (1902), in Gifford, *Leo Tolstoy*, p. 113.

Defamiliarization, or 'looking at things afresh'

Viktor Shklovsky discusses defamiliarization (*ostranenie*) in 'Art as Technique' in *Russian Formalist Criticism: Four Essays*, trans. Lee T. Lemon and Marian J. Reis (Lincoln: U of Nebraska Press, 1965), pp. 3–24. Edward Howard Crosby comments on Tolstoy's 'habit of looking at things afresh' in *Tolstoy and his Message* (London: Arthur C. Fifield, Simple Life Press, 1904), p. 13; Vinokenty Veresaev explains Tolstoy's 'device' of describing a phenomenon 'simply the way it is', in: *Zhivaia zhizn'* (Moscow: I. N. Kushnerov, 1911), vol. 1, p. 116.

Depicting inner life

Dmitry Pisarev wrote of Tolstoy's ability to report on the workings of the soul in an 1859 review, 'Tri smerti. Rasskaz grafa L. N. Tolstogo', in *L. N. Tolstoi v russkoi kritike* (Moscow: Khud. lit., 1952), pp. 132–3. Virginia Woolf comments on Tolstoy's ability to read minds in 'The Cossacks', *Essays*, ed. Andrew McNeillie (San Diego: Harcourt Brace Jovanovich, 1989–91), vol. 2, pp. 77–9.

Time and plot

Woolf's comments on Tolstoy's stories not 'shut[ting] with a snap' are also in 'The Cossacks', pp. 77–9. Tolstoy's draft for the foreword to *War and Peace* is excerpted in Gifford, *Leo Tolstoy*, pp. 38–9.

Simile and the power of comparison

George Steiner explores Homeric features of Tolstoy's work in *Tolstoy or Dostoevsky: An Essay in the Old Criticism* (New York:

Dutton, 1971). For Nabokov on Tolstoy's similes, see *Lectures on Russian Literature* (New York: Harcourt Brace, 1981), p. 202.

Hidden symmetries

Percy Lubbock discusses Tolstoy's reliance on 'pictorial contrast' in *The Craft of Fiction* (New York: Viking, 1957), pp. 235–50. Theodore Roosevelt commented on the barely connected plots of *Anna Karenina* in a letter of 12 April 1886. Boris Eikhenbaum writes of the 'dotted line' between the plots in: *Tolstoi in the Seventies*, trans. Albert Kaspin (Ann Arbor: Ardis, 1982), p. 111. Tolstoy explained the hidden 'architectonics' of *Anna Karenina* in a letter to S. A. Rachinskii of 27 January 1878 (63:377).

Chapter 8: Tolstoy cannot be silent

Defamiliarizing the hanging of men

As he defines defamiliarization, Shklovsky notes that it is 'typical' of Tolstoy to use the device to 'prick at our conscience'. Viktor Shklovsky, 'Art as Technique', *Russian Formalist Criticism*, trans. Lee T. Lemon and Marion J. Reis (Lincoln, Nebr.: University of Nebraska Press, 1965), p. 13.

Further reading

Biographies

Bartlett, Rosamund. *Tolstoy: A Russian Life* (New York: Houghton Mifflin, 2013).

Maude, Aylmer. *Leo Tolstoy: The First Fifty Years* and *Leo Tolstoy: Later Years* (New York: Dodd, 1910–11).

Shklovsky, Viktor. *Leo Tolstoy,* trans. Olga Shartse (Moscow: Progress, 1978).

Simmons, Ernest J. *Leo Tolstoy* (Boston: Little, Brown and Company, 1946).

Wilson, A. N. *Tolstoy: A Biography* (New York: Norton, 1988).

Letters and diaries

Christian, R. F., ed. and trans. *Tolstoy's Letters* (New York: Scribner, 1978).

Christian, R. F., ed. and trans. *Tolstoy's Diaries* (New York: Scribner, 1985).

Porter, Cathy, ed. and trans. *Diaries of Sophia Tolstoy* (New York: Random House, 1985).

Critical anthologies

Gifford, Henry, ed. *Leo Tolstoy* (London: Penguin Critical Anthology, 1971).

Knowles, A. V., ed. *Tolstoy: The Critical Heritage* (London: Routledge & Kegan Paul, 1978).

Introductions

Christian, Reginald Frank. *Tolstoy: A Critical Introduction* (Cambridge: Cambridge UP, 1969).

Gifford, Henry. *Tolstoy* (Oxford: Oxford UP, 1982).

Love, Jeff. *Tolstoy: A Guide for the Perplexed* (London: Continuum, 2008).

Orwin, Donna Tussing, ed. *The Cambridge Companion to Tolstoy* (Cambridge: Cambridge UP, 2002).

Orwin, Donna Tussing. *Simply Tolstoy* (New York: Simply Charly, 2017).

Critical studies and collections that span a range of works

Bayley, John. *Tolstoy and the Novel* (Chicago: U Chicago P, 1966).

Berman, Anna A. *Siblings in Tolstoy and Dostoevsky: The Path of Universal Brotherhood* (Evanston, Ill.: Northwestern UP, 2015).

Christian, Reginald Frank and Jones, Malcolm V., eds. *New Essays on Tolstoy* (Cambridge: Cambridge UP, 1978).

Hruska, Anne. 'Love and Slavery: Serfdom, Emancipation, and Family in Tolstoy's Fiction', *The Russian Review*, Vol. 66, No. 4 (Oct. 2007), pp. 627–46.

McLean, Hugh. *In Quest of Tolstoy* (Boston: Academic Studies Press, 2008).

Orwin, Donna Tussing, ed. *Anniversary Essays on Tolstoy* (Cambridge: Cambridge UP, 2010).

Steiner, George. *Tolstoy or Dostoevsky: An Essay in the Old Criticism* (New York: Dutton, 1971).

Weir, Justin. *Leo Tolstoy and the Alibi of Narrative* (New Haven: Yale UP, 2010).

Studies of particular works and periods

Early works (before *War and Peace*)

Allen, Elizabeth Cheresh, ed. *Before They Were Titans: Essays on the Early Works of Dostoevsky and Tolstoy* (Boston: Academic Studies Press, 2015).

Eikhenbaum, Boris. *The Young Tolstoy*, trans. Garry Kern (Ann Arbor: Ardis, 1982).

Williams, Gareth. *Tolstoy's 'Childhood'* (London: Bristol Classical Press, 1995).

War and Peace

Berlin, Isaiah. *The Hedgehog and the Fox* (New York: Simon & Schuster, 1986 [1953]).

Bloom, Harold, ed. *Leo Tolstoy's War and Peace* (New York: Chelsea House, 1988), esp. Robert Louis Jackson, 'The Second Birth of Pierre Bezukhov'.

Eikenbaum, Boris. *Tolstoi in the Sixties,* trans. Duffield White (Ann Arbor: Ardis, 1982).

Feuer, Kathryn B. *Tolstoy and the Genesis of War and Peace*, ed. Robin Feuer Miller and Donna Tussing Orwin (Ithaca, NY: Cornell UP, 1996).

McPeak, Rick and Orwin, Donna Tussing, eds. *Tolstoy on War: Narrative Art and Historical Truth in War and Peace* (Ithaca, NY: Cornell UP, 2012).

Morson, Gary Saul. *Hidden in Plain View: Narrative and Creative Potentials in War and Peace* (Stanford, Calif.: Stanford UP, 1987).

Anna Karenina

Alexandrov, Vladimir. *Limits to Interpretation: The Meanings of 'Anna Karenina'* (Madison: University of Wisconsin Press, 2004).

Eikhenbaum, Boris. *Tolstoi in the Seventies,* trans. A. Kaspin (Ann Arbor: Ardis, 1982).

Jackson, Robert Louis. 'Breaking the Moral Barrier' and 'Chance and Design: Anna Karenina's First Meeting with Vronsky', in *Close Encounters: Essays on Russian Literature* (Boston:Academic Studies Press, 2013).

Knapp, Liza, and Mandelker, Amy, eds. *Approaches to Teaching Tolstoy's 'Anna Karenina'* (New York: Modern Language Association Publications, 2003).

Knapp, Liza. *Anna Karenina and Others: Tolstoy's Labyrinth of Plots* (Madison: U of Wisconsin P, 2016).

Kokobobo, Ani, and Lieber, Emma, eds. *'Anna Karenina' for the Twenty-First Century* (DeLand, Fla: Tolstoy Studies Journal, 2016).

Mandelker, Amy. *Framing 'Anna Karenina': Tolstoy, the Woman Question, and the Victorian Novel* (Columbus, Oh.: Ohio State UP, 1993).

Morson, Gary Saul. *'Anna Karenina' in our Time: Seeing More Wisely* (New Haven: Yale UP, 2007).

Later fiction (after *Anna Karenina*)

Herman, David. 'Khadzhi-Murat's Silence', *Slavic Review*, Vol. 64, No. 1 (Spring 2005), pp. 1–23.

Jahn, Gary. *The Death of Ivan Ilich: An Interpretation* (New York: Twayne, 1993).

Katz, Michael, trans. and ed. *The Kreutzer Sonata Variations: Leo Tolstoy's Novella and Counterstories by Sophiya Tolstaya and Lev Lvovich Tolstoy* (New Haven: Yale UP, 2014).

Kokobobo, Ani. 'The Gentry Milieu as Grotesque Microcosm in Tolstoy's *Resurrection*', in *Russian Grotesque Realism* (Columbus, Oh.: Ohio State Press, 2018), ch. 5, pp. 98–116.

McLean, Hugh. *Resurrection*, in *The Cambridge Companion to Tolstoy* (Cambridge: Cambridge UP, 2002).

Moller, Peter Ulf. *Postlude to 'The Kreutzer Sonata': Tolstoj and the Debate on Sexual Morality in Russian Literature in the 1890s* (Leiden: Brill Academic, 1988).

Tolstoy beyond fiction: action, thought, belief, self-writing, death

Alston, Charlotte. *Tolstoy and his Disciples: The History of a Radical International Movement* (London: I. B. Tauris, 2014).

Blaisdell, Bob. *Tolstoy as Teacher: Tolstoy's Writings on Education* (New York: Teachers and Writers Collaborative, 2000).

Cracraft, James. *Two Shining Souls: Jane Addams, Leo Tolstoy, and the Quest for Global Peace* (Lanham, Md: Lexington Books, 2012).

Crosby, Ernest Howard. *Tolstoy as Schoolmaster* (London: Arthur Fifield, Simple Life Press, 1904).

Green, Martin, *Tolstoy and Gandhi: Men of Peace* (New York: Harper Collins, 1999).

Gustafson, Richard F. *Leo Tolstoy: Resident and Stranger. A Study in Fiction and Theology* (Princeton: Princeton UP, 1986).

McLean, Hugh. 'Tolstoy and Jesus' in *In Quest of Tolstoy* (Boston: Academic Studies Press, 2008), pp. 117–42.

Marks, Steven G. *How Russia Shaped the Modern World: From Art to Anti-Semitism, Ballet to Bolshevism* (Princeton: Princeton UP, 2003), ch. 4, pp. 102–39.

Medzhibovskaya, Inessa. *Tolstoy and the Religious Culture of his Time: A Biography of a Long Conversion, 1845–1887* (Lanham, Md: Lexington Books, 2009).

Nickel, William. *The Death of Tolstoy: Russia on the Eve, Astapovo Station, 1910* (Ithaca, NY, & London: Cornell UP, 2010).

Orwin, Donna Tussing. *Tolstoy's Art and Thought: 1847–1889* (Princeton: Princeton UP, 1993).

Paperno, Irina. *'Who, What Am I?' Tolstoy Struggles to Narrate the Self* (Ithaca, NY: Cornell UP, 2014).

Index

Leo Tolstoy